PRAYERS,

Bud ~~~~~ 2018

Especially for

_____

From

_____

Date

_____

PRAYERS

and

PROMISES

for Fathers

BARBOUR
PUBLISHING

To Adam, Sydney, Samuel, Matthew, Megan, and Christian

Published by Barbour Publishing, Inc., P.O. Box 719, Uhrichsville, Ohio 44683, www.barbourbooks.com

Our mission is to publish and distribute inspirational products offering exceptional value and biblical encouragement to the masses.

Member of the
Evangelical Christian
Publishers Association

Printed in China.

CONTENTS

...

PREFACE

■ ■ ■

The thought-provoking prayers on these pages are written especially for dads, from a dad's perspective. The prayers appeal to the emotion as well as the intellect and draw the heart and mind closer to God by expressing thanksgiving, happiness, patience, and obedience.

All prayers begin with a scripture quotation. The verses are compelling reminders that God promises to bless dads who speak to Him with humility and live faithfully. As the Bible directs, "Listen, children, to a father's instruction, and be attentive, that you may gain insight; for I give you good precepts: do not forsake my teaching" (Proverbs 4:1–2 NRSV).

ASPIRATIONS

TARGET

*With this in mind, we constantly pray for you,
that our God may make you worthy of his calling,
and that by his power he may bring to fruition
your every desire for goodness and your
every deed prompted by faith.*

2 THESSALONIANS 1:11 NIV

■ ■ ■

Father, I've seen people who have chosen a goal for their life's work when they were young and reached their target as straight as an arrow shot by a skilled archer. I've seen others follow a long and tortuous path to their eventual goal. Sometimes parents who try to live their children's lives for them have caused the deviation.

Lord, it is a fine line that I must follow in helping my children decide upon a career. Give me the parenting skill to direct rather than suppress the aspirations of my children. You have plans for them. Help me overcome excessive caution that may influence them to miss the opportunities that You are opening for them.

Father, I pray that we will search Your Word, pray, and listen to Your voice to learn what You have in mind for us. Help us be flexible enough to allow Your hands to mold us.

GOALS

And that ye study to be quiet, and to do your own business,
and to work with your own hands, as we commanded you;
That ye may walk honestly toward them that are without,
and that ye may have lack of nothing.
1 THESSALONIANS 4:11–12 KJV

■ ■ ■

Father, I need to have aspirations. Left without goals, I would only feed my desire for pleasure. Help me gain an understanding of Your will for me. Give me insight and guide me to problems worthy of attack.

Lord, sometimes the clutter of my life blocks my aspirations. At other times, I am too easily persuaded that my goals cannot be reached or that an easier way will lead to success. Help me be an example to my children of a purpose-driven life.

Father, I want to have a life in which I strive to meet my goals. But I pray that I do not become so overwhelmed with my aspirations that I betray my Christian disposition. I've seen people who undertake an important task and become obsessed with success. They become belligerent with anyone who doesn't share their vision. They exercise brutal force over anyone who dares to disagree with them. As I press ahead, help me remain cheerful, even-tempered, and polite.

GROWTH

*Let us therefore follow after the things
which make for peace, and things
wherewith one may edify another.*
ROMANS 14:19 KJV

■ ■ ■

Father, I realize that some goals cannot be achieved, but they are worth the effort anyway. By accepting the challenge, I grow and gain abilities that I would not develop otherwise. I do not know in my own life where difficulty ends and the impossible begins. But I pray that I'll continue to strive for excellence even when the prospects are against me.

Lord, I pray that my children will pursue their dreams, too. Help us aim high. Even if we do not succeed, help us grow because of the attempt. Please help us live lives that make a difference.

Father, guide me to recognize the fact that the Bible addresses all of my hopes and fears. It guides me to the goals to which I should aspire. May I help my children see that their lives will be richer by following the course that brings them closer to Your perfection.

Achievement

■ ■ ■

Father, I want to be an achiever, although I do not always
understand where my real talents lie. I often begin projects but let my enthusiasm for them grow cold when I see
that I am unlikely to develop a superior ability at them. I
realize, too late, that I have invested time and effort into a
project that did not have Your blessing.

Lord, help me grasp the fact that my greatest efforts should be directed toward how I lead my life as a
Christian. Please guide me to goals that are worthy of my
efforts—goals that will bring satisfaction because I am
doing them for You.

Father, remind me that my aspirations should not be
for skill at an established occupation or success in a specific undertaking. Instead, my aim should be to prepare
myself to be a good leader of my family and for whatever
other jobs You have in mind for me.

Time

*I have shewed you all things, how that so labouring ye ought
to support the weak, and to remember the words of the Lord
Jesus, how he said, It is more blessed to give than to receive.*
ACTS 20:35 KJV

■ ■ ■

Father, upon my return from a business trip, my young
children asked me to play, and it took a determined effort
to do so because I had spent all of my energy at work. I
realize that if I do not play with my little ones while I have
them, they will soon spring up, and then the opportunity
will be lost. I can constantly pursue my business only at
the neglect of many other things, including my family.

Lord, help me recognize the importance of devoting a
special portion of my time to play with my children. They
need quality time, but unless I provide the quantity, I will
not be there when the special need arises.

Father, when my children were learning to walk, I
would hold them to keep them from falling. Now they are
older, but they still need my time and support to assure
their success at other endeavors. Help me prepare them
for the future.

PRESENCE IN MIND

*"Now my eyes will be open and my ears attentive to the
prayer that is made in this place. For now I have chosen
and consecrated this house so that my name may be there
forever; my eyes and my heart will be there for all time."*
2 CHRONICLES 7:15–16 NRSV

∎ ∎ ∎

Lord, when I am with my children, I am always conscious
that I am a father. My actions more readily conform to
what I should do and say. I am kinder, more affectionate,
and ever helpful. I take seriously my duty to guide, discipline, and teach how they should conduct themselves.
Help me realize that even when they are not in my presence, my duties as a father do not cease. As the head of
my family, I represent them to the community. I am paving
the way for them.

Father, I pray, too, that I will influence my children for
good even when they are not in my presence. Help them
see my smile, listen to my words, and follow my guidance.
I pray that my influence persists even when I am physically absent. Dear Father, help me also be mindful of Your
presence in my life.

PRESENCE

*And he said, My presence shall go
with thee, and I will give thee rest.*
EXODUS 33:14 KJV

❋ ❋ ❋

Father, I know that a situation becomes worse when the mind is troubled. But support and encouragement can overcome bleak times. Sometimes my role as father is merely to be there.

While my daughter was doing volunteer work at the hospital, she was accused of taking a piece of jewelry. When I arrived and stood at her side, my presence gave her confidence. With cool and convincing words, she stated her innocence. I am thankful that a short time later a relative of the patient notified the hospital that the item had been found where it had been placed for safekeeping.

To my daughter, it was not the number of people who stood by her side, but her confidence in the one who did. Heavenly Father, how great You are because You stand by me despite my shortcomings. I know Your presence upholds me in the face of strong opposition. Help me emulate You in being there for my family.

Never Resign

*"Lord, the God of our fathers Abraham, Isaac and Israel. . .
give my son Solomon the wholehearted devotion to keep
your commands, statutes and decrees."*
1 Chronicles 29:18–19 niv

■ ■ ■

Father, as children enter their teenage years, the choices
they make can have impact far greater than when they
were younger. At this stage in their lives, there are many
hazardous attitudes that I could take. I could become
overbearing with a "Follow the rules, or else!" attitude. Or,
at any hint of problem, I could overreact quickly, without
thinking. I may incorrectly believe it is impossible for them
to do wrong because I've trained them so well. I've also
seen fathers who resign as parents at this stage because
they no longer think they can make a difference.

Lord, help me realize that I can make a difference.
I must not abdicate my responsibilities as a father merely
because the task has become more difficult. Help me
guide my teenagers to accurately perceive the right
choices and the true way based on Your Word.

ACCEPTANCE

*May the God of hope fill you with all joy and
peace in believing, so that you may abound in
hope by the power of the Holy Spirit.*
ROMANS 15:13 NRSV

■ ■ ■

Father, when I was a little child, I visited my grandmother
who had this soft, down-filled feather bed. On a chilly
morning, I would sink into it and be toasty warm. Grandma
called it a comforter. I thought the name fit exactly because it gave me a pleasant, secure feeling.

Lord, I can still use a spiritual comforter. It usually
happens when the chill of self-doubt attacks me. I give up
on myself. I think I'll never learn how to successfully complete an assignment, or that when it is complete, a glaring
error will be visible. I fear that those who depend on me
will turn away in disappointment.

Lord, I often see this same insecurity in my children. I
am astonished at how critical they can be of themselves.
I realize now the importance of the comfort of Your Holy
Spirit. Help us all remember that You accept us regardless of our shortcomings.

CONNECTION

*Am I now trying to win the approval of human beings,
or of God? Or am I trying to please people? If I were still
trying to please people, I would not be a servant of Christ.*
GALATIANS 1:10 NIV

■ ■ ■

Father, at one time I did not fully commit myself to You. I
sought to associate with others whom I imagined would
fill my need to belong. I scheduled group activities, joined
clubs, and found hobbies I could share with others. Yet
these did not bring the sense of belonging that I sought.
Even with the swirl of activity around me, I felt empty and
isolated. The connection to others only became satisfying
after I first connected to You.

Lord, I've seen young people who think glitz, frantic
activities, and mindless pursuits will fill a void in their
lives. I can understand their desperate search because I
have felt it, too. But I no longer have an incessant worry
about belonging because I belong to You, and that is
enough. I pray that I have shown my children that a better
life comes simply from being close to You.

Support

*"Take my yoke upon you, and learn from me; for I am gentle
and humble in heart, and you will find rest for your souls.
For my yoke is easy, and my burden is light."*
MATTHEW 11:29–30 NRSV

■ ■ ■

Father, an outdoor magazine recommended using a hiking stick to make hiking easier. The extra support would prevent falling when negotiating a difficult, rock-strewn trail. But I refused to accept that the aid of a hiking stick would benefit me. In my stubbornness, I decided to ignore the advice and avoid the extra bother of carrying a stick. I wanted to do it myself and be self-reliant.

Lord, I often fall into the deception of thinking that I do not need anything to lean on in my spiritual life. But my traverse of this life is filled with difficulties far more dangerous than an uneven trail. Help me put aside the misconception that I need no one but myself. Help me develop the humility to recognize that I need to lean on You.

Father, I pray that neither my family nor I ever stand so sure of ourselves that we think we can never stumble. May we always be willing to seek Your comfort and support.

REFUGE

God is our refuge and strength, an ever-present help in trouble. Therefore we will not fear, though the earth give way and the mountains fall into the heart of the sea.
PSALM 46:1–2 NIV

■ ■ ■

Father, I've read that some animals in Africa become frightened at the sound of the lion's powerful roar. Often they are in a brush pile where they have perfect safety. But they bolt from their cover, and in their confusion they run toward the lion rather than away from it.

Lord, the evil desires in my life—anger, envy, covetousness, and addictions—are constantly trying to pull me from my place of safety with You. I must keep You clearly in mind as my place of refuge. Otherwise, when dangerous desires call me, I might run the wrong way. It is not enough to merely rid my life of these wicked attractions. I must anchor my heart in Your love.

Father, I pray that my children will learn the importance of knowing that You are their shelter. By reading the Bible, praying, developing Christian friendships, and obeying You, they will have protection from the world's evil intentions.

COMMITMENT

EQUIPPED

May the God of peace. . .equip you with everything
good for doing his will, and may he work in us what
is pleasing to him, through Jesus Christ, to whom
be glory for ever and ever. Amen.
HEBREWS 13:20–21 NIV

■ ■ ■

Father, as I grew up, my father experienced terrible economic conditions. Every day was a financial struggle, and he did not have the advantage of a network of supportive family members. At times, it must have been a severe temptation to give up. But he embraced You rather than the world. He never abdicated his duties as a father.

Heavenly Father, I've seen supervisors in the place where I work be promoted to positions for which they are ill suited. They have the luxury of delegating those tasks in which they are incompetent to others. But a good father cannot give away his duties or decide that he no longer wants to be a father. He must continue.

Lord, bless me so I will have the patience and dedication to be a first-rate father. Open my eyes to Your Word so I see those scriptures that will equip me for my responsibilities in raising my children.

Genuine

Hide your face from my sins and blot out all my iniquity.
Create in me a pure heart, O God, and renew
a steadfast spirit within me.
PSALM 51:9–10 NIV

■ ■ ■

Father, when my children are sorry for some infraction
of the rules, I explain that the proof of their repentance
is their commitment to do better. It is not in their outward
show, which can be a sham, but in whether they make a
sincere effort to improve.

Lord, sometimes I find myself less than authentic
when I feign commitment to a worthy cause. I nod wisely,
readily agree that something needs to be done, and then
walk away and forget the matter entirely. Please forgive
me, and strengthen me so that my heart is without deceit.

Father, when I make a commitment, help me stand
behind it because it has my full and honest endorsement.
May I feel bound to bring the task to successful comple-
tion. Strengthen my resolve to be an example to my children of the importance of making a genuine effort to fulfill
commitments.

Primary Duty

That he would grant unto us, that we being
delivered out of the hand of our enemies
might serve him without fear, in holiness and
righteousness before him, all the days of our life.
LUKE 1:74–75 KJV

■ ■ ■

Father, my company requires me to investigate injuries on the job, determine the cause, and propose how to prevent the accident from happening again. In many cases, I've found that accidents occur when a person tries to accomplish two tasks at the same time. Neither one is done well. The balancing act of trying to satisfy two different goals leads to disaster. Accident victims often do not have a clear commitment to their primary task, and they become indecisive when they must choose between their main duty and a secondary function.

In Your Word, Lord, I read about the impossibility of serving two masters. I commit to You my time, talent, money, and my physical and emotional energy. I pray that I will be single-minded so that when a situation calls for action I will not hesitate to serve You. I pray that my children will recognize that decisions become easier once they develop the clear purpose to serve You first.

SELF-HELP

*For, "All people are like grass, and all their glory is like the
flowers of the field; the grass withers and the flowers fall,
but the word of the Lord endures forever." And this is
the word that was preached to you.*
1 PETER 1:24–25 NIV

■ ■ ■

Lord, around the office, I see people carrying self-help
books to read during their lunch break. Another title
makes the bestseller list each month. Yet few of these
books have enough substance to be enduring classics.

Heavenly Father, when I think about the makeup of
my personality, I find many constants—I am sinful, selfish,
full of pride, and sometimes afraid. My greatest concerns
are the inadequacies that I find in my character, especially those of being a family leader. And so, I am commit-
ted to taking the steps that will bring me closer to being a
good father.

Lord, the Bible addresses all these issues that I face.
Your Word is more thorough than any contemporary book
that tries to show me how to improve myself. May I always
remember to turn to Your enduring guidebook for daily
living and eternal salvation.

COMMUNICATION

MEANINGFUL

*Do not let any unwholesome talk come out of your mouths,
but only what is helpful for building others up according to
their needs, that it may benefit those who listen.*
EPHESIANS 4:29 NIV

. . .

Lord, I have seen relationships between husband and
wife and between father and children dissolve because
of a failure to communicate. The lack of an interchange
of thoughts and information caused erosion in the family
camaraderie.

I ask that You will help me to relate well with my wife
and children. May my conversation with them be more
than mere words. Help me express myself in a way that is
readily and clearly understood. Help me listen in such a
way that I hear not only the words of my children but also
the ideas and heartfelt concerns that they convey.

On a spiritual level, I pray that my heavenly communication keeps an open line. Help me to continually evaluate my relationship with You. Staying in contact with You,
Lord, has eternal importance to help me realize my blessings and translate them into actions to share with others.

POWER

In this way the word of the Lord
spread widely and grew in power.
ACTS 19:20 NIV

■ ■ ■

Father, I read well-known Bible stories such as the miracle of loaves and fishes to my little children. I am amazed at how the stories capture their minds. Sometimes they ask me to read same story over and over until they have it memorized.

Lord, for my own study, I am reading the book of Acts. Throughout it I find stories that range from Paul's emotional farewell at Ephesus to the exciting adventure of his shipwreck on the way to Rome.

Father, I am constantly amazed at the power of the Bible to touch the lives of people regardless of their age, education, or economic level. Long ago, shepherds and others with humble backgrounds first heard the simple parables spoken by Your Son. Today, the lives of well-educated city dwellers are being touched by the same parables. Father, may I continue to open my heart to the power of the Bible.

Daily

Rejoice always, pray without ceasing,
give thanks in all circumstances; for this
is the will of God in Christ Jesus for you.
1 Thessalonians 5:16–18 nrsv

■ ■ ■

Father, I have come into my room alone to spend some time with You. I am dismayed when I realize how much time has passed since we have talked without interruptions. I know I have spoken with You throughout the day, and that in doing so I had Your undivided attention. But my mind has been flooded with distractions, so my attentiveness wavers.

Lord, should my children come to me to discuss subjects of importance, I give them my full attention, and I expect them to do the same. Yet I often fail to allot uninterrupted time for prayer. Please forgive me.

Father, when I face a stressful interview at work, I rehearse in my mind what I am going to say. I polish the sentences until they express precisely what I mean. I am thankful, Lord, that I can come to You without rehearsal. Regardless of how poorly I express myself, You know the concerns that are on my mind. Help me to bring them to You every day.

REQUESTS

Be careful for nothing; but in every thing by prayer
and supplication with thanksgiving let your requests
be made known unto God. And the peace of God,
which passeth all understanding, shall keep your
hearts and minds through Christ Jesus.
PHILIPPIANS 4:6–7 KJV

■ ■ ■

Father, I am aware of many people who are suffering and
in difficult situations. I pray that they and their families
will be able to work out the difficulties. Help me to find a
way to help ease their burdens.

Father, sometimes my own children have problems,
but because of their lack of experience, they cannot express what is troubling them. Their distress can go un-
noticed unless I devote time to being with them and talking
with them. Guide me to giving them the support they need.
Help them realize that they can make their requests known
to me—and to You.

GENEROSITY

*"Give, and it will be given to you. A good measure,
pressed down, shaken together and running over,
will be poured into your lap. For with the measure
you use, it will be measured to you."*
LUKE 6:38 NIV

■ ■ ■

Lord, You set the standard for generosity by giving Your
life for a sinful world. May I always be reminded of Your
sacrifice when I see a need that I can serve. Just like a
farmer who plants seeds and profits from a harvest, You
also bless those who share their assets.

Lord, to show kindness, one must be thoughtful. One
of my son's friends had agreed to do extra chores for his
family. But when the friend became injured, my son volun-
teered to do the chores until his friend recovered. I appreciate the fact that my son thought beyond himself. Father,
please help me continue to encourage him to think about
others so his character will become even more generous.

Heavenly Father, also help me to give with a pure mo-
tive to bless those in need and not for the selfish reason
that I expect to be rewarded. I truly want to be Your hand
extended to help those who have physical, spiritual, and
financial needs.

Rescue

Inasmuch as ye have done it unto one of the least
of these my brethren, ye have done it unto me.
Matthew 25:40 KJV

■ ■ ■

Lord Jesus, I read in the Bible that when I come to the rescue of those who are hungry and thirsty, I am loving You. Help me never accept pain and suffering as a natural condition. Guide me to show the compassion that You had when You healed the sick and fed the hungry multitudes. Give me the ability to put sympathy into action for those who suffer.

Lord, help me overcome the thought that someone—whether acquaintance or stranger—is unworthy of compassion. May Your rich blessings fall upon my family and me so that we can be contributors of aid rather than recipients.

Heavenly Father, I thank You for Your continual watchful eye upon me. Guide me to bring a concrete expression of love to others who have a physical or emotional crisis. Provide me with the wisdom to relieve the suffering of others.

Mercy

*Be kind to one another, tenderhearted, forgiving
one another, as God in Christ has forgiven you.*
EPHESIANS 4:32 NRSV

■ ■ ■

Father, not only does compassion restore order to shattered lives, it brings people back from the brink of hopelessness. It is a catalyst that starts them on the road to recovery. Help me develop awareness of the distress of others and strengthen my determination to relieve it.

Lord, sometimes the fact that an acquaintance needs compassion creeps up on me—an aged neighbor, a relative who has become sick, a friend who is struggling with a chronic illness, a former coworker who has been unemployed. Help me recognize and respond to these very evident needs.

Father, I desire to be a more compassionate person. Help me be kind and forgiving. Give me a heart full of mercy. Help me identify those ways in which I can serve others. Guide me to enlist the assistance of my family so they learn how to serve You by helping others.

Strangers

*"Love your enemies, do good to those who hate you,
bless those who curse you, pray for those who abuse you.
Do to others as you would have them do to you."*
Luke 6:27–28, 31 NRSV

∙∙∙

Father, I know that compassion for others begins with an awareness of their suffering, followed by a desire to relieve it. But compassion is not complete until I take action. It is easy to follow my heart into action for close family members and for others who are important to me, but it is more difficult to help strangers.

Lord, I confess that even when I develop an impulse to help, I am reluctant to involve myself with those I do not know. Many needy individuals suffer situations so severe that I have difficulty even imagining what they must endure. I despair that my efforts would not have a lasting benefit.

Father, help me see people around me through Your caring eyes. Although I may not have the special skills to meet every need, give me the determination not to be afraid to be kind. Let me show mercy so that mercy will be mine when I come to You.

CONFIDENCE

Investment

And those who know your name put their trust in you,
for you, O Lord, have not forsaken those who seek you.
Psalm 9:10 nrsv

■ ■ ■

Father, each morning I read the business section of the newspaper. The economic future looks bright one day, but the next day projections are bleak. I carefully invest my meager resources, but the fluctuation of interest rates and an unstable stock market make me wary. None of the choices are completely free of risk. Things can go drastically wrong in a heartbeat.

Lord, I am unable to see what the future holds, but I trust You as the One who holds the future. Life's wealth often comes and goes, but my security is in You, my Provider.

Father, as my children grow and develop, their needs rapidly change. Provide me with the skills and resources I need to promote their continued growth. I invest my trust in You to guide me to meet the physical, emotional, and spiritual needs of my family. Help me make my first and most important investment in my family.

In God

May the God of hope fill you with all joy and peace
as you trust in him, so that you may overflow
with hope by the power of the Holy Spirit.
ROMANS 15:13 NIV

∎ ∎ ∎

Father, having confidence is easy when I am not under attack. It is only when I am belittled or ridiculed that my confidence can crumble. My wife and children love and respect me, and my friends encourage me, but the greatest security comes from trusting You.

Lord, I must not think that having wealth or power will give me confidence. Help me develop the calm confidence that comes from upholding righteous convictions. May my children see my example so they understand that confidence is void unless it is exercised for good.

Father, may I be faithful in putting my trust in You. May my prayers for strength to overcome difficulties always come from an honest heart. Protect me from wavering as I follow You.

TRUST

*Trust in the Lord with all thine heart; and lean
not unto thine own understanding. In all thy ways
acknowledge him, and he shall direct thy paths.*
PROVERBS 3:5–6 KJV

■ ■ ■

Father, when I first came to You, I was so determined to
do great works that I considered little jobs beneath my
effort. When I fell short of my goals, I despaired of ever doing anything for You. All along, a multitude of small deeds
had been available, but I ignored them.

Father, I am careful to give my children tasks within
their ability. For a more difficult assignment, I help them
move toward the final goal in easy stages. Should a problem arise, I am willing to step in and help them. They have
no reason to be apprehensive that they might fail. Soon
they can do the entire task on their own.

Lord, I realize now that in the little tasks You are preparing me for a larger mission. Grant me the eyes to see
little jobs that need to be done and the willing heart to do
them.

HUMILITY

*All of you must clothe yourselves with humility in
your dealings with one another, for "God opposes
the proud, but gives grace to the humble."*
1 PETER 5:5 NRSV

■ ■ ■

Father, sometimes I feel so uncertain of myself that I cannot achieve my goals because the slightest criticism or hint that I may be on the wrong path paralyzes me into inaction. At other times, I develop self-confidence but only generate it by thinking more highly of myself than I ought. In between the two extremes, I wish to develop calm confidence without the haughty attitude that befalls those who think they are always right.

Lord, may nothing in my manner suggest arrogance. Any success that I reap is because You planted the seed. I want to base my self-confidence not upon myself, but on the One I walk beside. My confidence is built when I welcome You into my heart and mind and lay myself bare before You.

Father, my trust is not in myself, but in You. Help me to lead my family with confidence.

JOURNEY

*I have learned the secret of being content in any
and every situation, whether well fed or hungry,
whether living in plenty or in want. I can do
all this through him who gives me strength.*
PHILIPPIANS 4:12–13 NIV

■ ■ ■

Dear Lord, when I was a child, my father drove along a road where a rainbow seemed to end just over the next hill. But no matter how far we traveled, we never reached the end of the rainbow. It was always ahead of us.

Father, as an adult I have set many goals that I thought would bring contentment if I could only achieve them. But I discovered that no matter what I achieved, contentment stayed out of reach. Thank You for showing me that contentment is not a destination but the way I make my journey.

Lord, help me set worthy goals and encourage my children to do the same. But also guide us to set goals based on what You want us to do rather than what we imagine will bring pleasure, success, and contentment. Instead of looking forward in discontent for better situations, let us focus on what You have given us. May we see our cup as running over with Your blessings.

PRESTIGE

But godliness with contentment is great gain. For we brought nothing into this world, and it is certain we can carry nothing out. And having food and raiment let us be therewith content.
1 TIMOTHY 6:6–8 KJV

■ ■ ■

Heavenly Father, as a teenager, I dreamed of owning a big, four-wheel-drive pickup truck. I imagined how it would impress the girl who took my order in the drive-through at the fast-food restaurant. Today, I smile at those juvenile attempts to get the attention of someone whose name I can no longer remember.

Father, I pray that my children will develop good judgment of what is important. But I must continually remind myself to do so, too, because I still find myself trying to impress people. I sometimes engage in silly, immature behavior as I chase empty prestige and status. I still fall into the trap of trying to impress people by my possessions.

Lord, I humbly pray that I will be content with the blessings You give. Help me focus my thoughts on living a dedicated life. Remind me that the things that I own do not define me. Almighty God, I am delighted to have You as my Provider.

SIMPLICITY

*But I fear, lest by any means, as the serpent
beguiled Eve through his subtilty, so your minds should
be corrupted from the simplicity that is in Christ.*
2 CORINTHIANS 11:3 KJV

■ ■ ■

Lord, the management principle known as KISS—"Keep It Simple, Stupid"—does have its merit, despite the "Stupid" reference. I am involved in far too many organizations and other activities that fritter away my time and litter my mind. When did I agree to associate with so many organizations? Why did I subscribe to so many magazines? How many hobbies does one person need?

Father, I long for simplicity in my relationship with You. Please help me manage my time so I can focus on a better kinship with You. Release me from the clutter of unimportant activities that infringe on my time and attention.

Lord, I will monitor the activities of my children so that they do not become overloaded with activities that intrude on their time to grow spiritually. I pray that we will make quiet time for reflection and quality time for communicating with You.

ACTION

Little children, let us love, not in word
or speech, but in truth and action.
1 JOHN 3:18 NRSV

■ ■ ■

Dear Father, I pray that I will never be satisfied with
myself or become comfortable in my situation. May my
contentment be one of action instead of ease. Often responsibilities to my wife and children require prompt and
decisive action. I must not be lured into inaction as a crisis
develops.

Lord, I ask You to show me the doors of opportunity
that I can open to grow and improve. Should I refuse to
open those doors, then jar me out of my routine and force
me out of my comfort zone. When I see what needs to be
done, may I willingly make the effort to do it.

Father, I often see that change is necessary for me to
improve. If I do exactly the same thing each day in exactly
the same way, then I should not expect results any different from the day before. Help me push beyond the mundane into the realm of active service.

COUNSELOR

Responsibility

"God is exalted in his power.
Who is a teacher like him?"
Job 36:22 NIV

■ ■ ■

Lord, the opportunity to shape young lives is both a blessing and an awesome responsibility. Show me how to admonish, correct, and inspire those who look to me for guidance. Although I have opportunities to give advice to a variety of individuals at work, at church, and in the community, my greatest desire is to guide the minds of my children. Help me build relationships founded on trust.

Lord, no one teaches like You. Regardless of the circumstances, I will ground my advice on Your Word. Give me the dedication and calm self-assurance to help the people I am mentoring to realize the higher objectives for their lives. As a father, my influence will persist through the lives of my children. I pray that they will have the conviction to remain on course when I am no longer guiding them.

LIVING THE LIFE

For thou, Lord, art good, and ready to forgive;
and plenteous in mercy unto all them that call upon thee.
PSALM 86:5 KJV

■ ■ ■

Lord, it is easy to justify my own mistakes. Yet I find it difficult to ignore the shortcomings of others. When I am late getting ready, it is always for a good reason. But when my children delay getting ready and miss the bus, I lecture them on their indifference to their responsibilities. I have heard that ten praises are needed for every one criticism. Often, I provide the opposite.

Father, I can always detect problems in others more easily than in myself. That is the way my thinking goes, and I know it is not right. Help me to stop being reproachful of others while excusing my own inadequacy. Help me learn to weave my counsel into the fabric of my own life so others can see it.

With Your help, I will show my family and others the same tolerance You have shown me. By forgiving others, I accept Your free grace.

TEAMWORK

As every man hath received the gift,
even so minister the same one to another,
as good stewards of the manifold grace of God.
1 PETER 4:10 KJV

■ ■ ■

Lord Most High, I sometimes allow my future to be determined by others. I become dependent upon them to guide me and take the lead in overcoming my problems. At other times, I try to be totally independent of others and chart my own course. I fail to recognize that You have made human beings to be interdependent. I understand this concept as it applies to the church, to my marriage, and to my family.

Lord, may I also recognize the advantages of shared action in my daily contact with other people. By exchanging ideas and working together, we'll be more effective.

I pray that I do not think that in order for me to win, others must lose. Instead, guide me to succeed in cooperative endeavors that bring glory to Your kingdom. Bless my children with a spirit of teamwork. Let them use the gifts You have given them to benefit others.

Choices

I press on toward the goal to win the prize for which
God has called me heavenward in Christ Jesus.
PHILIPPIANS 3:14 NIV

∎ ∎ ∎

Father, last year a friend and I set out to hike a mountain trail. We had no particular destination in mind. The grueling trail ended in a field of boulders and an impassable bank of snow. Later, we learned of a different route that would have taken us to a spectacular vista at the summit.

Lord, I often expend my strength to reach an unworthy goal. The end result is often disappointing. My aim in life is to honor You. Guide me to make good decisions at work and at home. Help me to focus on the spiritual goals that will honor You.

Father, teach me how to use my time and resources wisely so I will be a good example for my children. Help me guide them so they will make excellent choices for their lives and strive for worthy goals.

PERSISTENCE

*For everything that was written in the past
was written to teach us, so that through the
endurance taught in the Scriptures and the
encouragement they provide we might have hope.*
ROMANS 15:4 NIV

■ ■ ■

Father, I often battle my computer, especially when installing a new peripheral. Nothing seems to work the first time! I change the data cable, plug it into a different port, reinstall the software, load new drivers, and even read the manual to learn the correct menu choices and commands. Eventually, it works.

Lord, every day I learn the effectiveness of persistence. I encounter problems that at first resist all of my efforts to overcome. But persistence prevails when all else fails. The greatest resistance by the forces against me comes at the moment before success.

Father, I see people who show simple persistence every day—the heroism of working at a thankless job, the endurance of a parent who must repeat the same tasks every day, the determination of a teenager to overcome physical or mental limitations. Grant me persistence and a steadfast singleness of purpose in raising my children and leading my family.

Pursuance

We sent Timothy, our brother and co-worker for God
in proclaiming the gospel of Christ, to strengthen and
encourage you for the sake of your faith, so that no
one would be shaken by these persecutions.
1 Thessalonians 3:2–3 nrsv

■ ■ ■

Father, I enjoy reading about great achievers in world history—statesmen, scientists, missionaries, and explorers. Many were people of exceptional courage, endurance, and intelligence. Yet my greatest admiration is for common people in extraordinary circumstances. They stepped out in faith and did what was required of them. Often, they did not seem to have great courage, but were willing to overcome their fears for a noble purpose. They were surprisingly eloquent, not in their words, but in their lives.

Lord, may I pursue worthy goals as an outgrowth of my Christian values. I desire to first establish in my heart the right choices and then follow them in my everyday life despite adversity. I pray that I will remain faithful to those values and be willing to submerge my own will to do Your will.

Father, help me steer my children toward real heroes, those who pursue righteousness. Encourage my children to be heroic in upholding the values that reflect Your will.

Resolution

But Daniel purposed in his heart that he would not defile himself with the portion of the king's meat, nor with the wine which he drank: therefore he requested of the prince of the eunuchs that he might not defile himself.
Daniel 1:8 KJV

∎ ∎ ∎

Heavenly Father, despite the quiet time my family is experiencing now, I know that challenges will test each one of us—if not later today, then sometime soon. Once temptations come, I seldom have adequate time or the proper environment to make a reasoned response. My goal is to look ahead and consider the evils I will face and make the right decision before the events occur. I wish also to foresee challenges my children will encounter and prepare them for those tests.

I pray that the choices I make will provide an example to my children so that they, too, will have the courage to choose truth over lies, courage over flight, righteousness over evil.

After I make an important decision, there is a time of second-guessing, both from myself and from others. Rid my mind of these doubts that serve no useful end. I pray I will be resolute and boldly live a consistent, purposeful life.

WISDOM

*The mouths of the righteous utter wisdom,
and their tongues speak justice. The law of their
God is in their hearts; their steps do not slip.*
PSALM 37:30–31 NRSV

...

Father, my knowledge is limited and my ignorance is end-less. Even when I know what should be done, I sometimes am faint of heart. I hesitate because I realize that my decisions often have consequences that will have major effects on my family.

Lord, I will never know enough to always make the right choices on my own. I pray that You will give me the wisdom to choose what is right and lasting. Give me the good sense to correctly discern the choices that keep me in agreement with Your eternal plan.

Father, let me show that I have Your blessing by leading an honorable and acceptable life. It is not always apparent to others that the best course of action is one in keeping with Your direction. Help me have the courage to act upon the wisdom that You have generously given me.

DISCIPLINE

INSTRUCTION

*No discipline seems pleasant at the time, but painful.
Later on, however, it produces a harvest of righteousness
and peace for those who have been trained by it.*
HEBREWS 12:11 NIV

■ ■ ■

Father, during one of my periodic attempts to improve my
golf game, an instructor watched my swing and offered
advice. His greatest concern was with my grip. He showed
me the proper way to place my thumb and fingers. He
insisted I use the new grip, although I found it uncomfort-
able at first.

Lord, I recognize that discipline is training that al-
ters a person's behavior for the better. May I always use
discipline to instruct, train, and teach my children. Give
me the temperament to handle anger so that anger and
punishment do not become part of my discipline. May my
discipline always be moderated with affection.

Father, it is difficult to overcome early training that is
bad, and it is difficult to go against early training that is
good. Help me give proper training that will last a lifetime.
Allow me to show my children the proof of my love for
them through discipline that sets their lives on the proper
course.

TESTS

Test them all;
hold on to what is good.
1 THESSALONIANS 5:21 NIV

■ ■ ■

Father, while going through school, teachers were always giving tests to students. I didn't like taking exams, but they did make me study the information being taught and motivate me to learn. Without periodic checks on my progress, I would have become careless in my studies and uncertain of my real mastery of the subject.

Lord, may I not become lax in learning more about You and living a life pleasing to You. When I am tested, help me make the choices that will lead to victory. As my children face decisions about proper spiritual choices, give me the talent to assist them when it is necessary and the wisdom to let them test their own mettle when it is appropriate.

Father, throughout life I encounter choices that challenge me. As I examine each situation, I pray that my desire will be to do what is right, and You will give me the strength to stand by my choice.

GEMS

Ye also, as lively stones, are built up a spiritual house,
an holy priesthood, to offer up spiritual sacrifices,
acceptable to God by Jesus Christ.
1 PETER 2:5 KJV

■ ■ ■

Lord, when I walk along a fast flowing stream or stand at the beach as the waves roll in, I am amazed at the ceaseless action of the water. I find stones that are rounded smooth by the continuous pounding of the water. Even the edges of broken glass are smoothed away until they are no longer sharp.

Father, I see Your ceaseless action in my life in the same way. Day by day, You remove my rough edges. You blunt my sharp tongue, soften my overbearing manner, cool my hot temper, and smooth out my uneven disposition. From a rough and unremarkable stone, You have made me into something better. Thank You for continuously changing me.

Heavenly Father, my children are also rough stones, but they have the potential to be gems. I pray I'll expose them to the right actions that will improve their character. Shape them into citizens of Your heavenly kingdom.

Consequences

Because the LORD disciplines those he loves,
as a father the son he delights in.
PROVERBS 3:12 NIV

■ ■ ■

Father, I have many roles in my position as the head of my
family. I approach discipline with more trepidation than
any other aspect of being a father. Most discipline is training—guiding the young one toward a specific goal. I put
rules in place to ensure that my children do not stray too
far from the expected pattern for their lives. But occasionally, the rules are intentionally broken and consequences
must be exacted.

Lord, help me choose realistic expectations and state
them clearly. Give me the wisdom to set the consequences
appropriate to the age of the child. A two-minute timeout
is an eternity for a small child. A two-week loss of the
phone is forever for a teenager. Despite their pleadings
and objections, help me enforce the consequences of the
rules I have set. Afterward, I pray that my children recognize the discipline as an indication of my love for them.

REVITALIZE

"But charge Joshua, and encourage and strengthen him,
because it is he who shall cross over at the head
of this people and who shall secure their possession
of the land that you will see."
DEUTERONOMY 3:28 NRSV

■ ■ ■

Father, You instructed Moses to encourage Joshua to lead Your people across the Jordan River into the Promised Land. In the same way, help me encourage those who have been chosen to serve. Help me ease their burdens and give them the will to continue the work You have called them to do.

Lord, when I am leading my family, may I always be mindful of my role as Your servant. Help me choose the right words and actions to revitalize my wife and children when they have grown weary, assure them when they have doubts, console them in times of apparent failure, and reward them with heartfelt praise for their successes. May I never ask them to do what I am unwilling to do myself.

Father, grant me the ability to choose what is right and give me the ability to persuade others to make that choice, too.

REFRESHED

*"I know your deeds, your love and faith,
your service and perseverance, and that you
are now doing more than you did at first."*
REVELATION 2:19 NIV

■ ■ ■

Father, when I awake each morning, I am rested, re-freshed, and ready to meet the challenges of the new day. But such a positive outlook is difficult to maintain all day long. When I become spiritually low, I am reminded to renew myself with You. I need to draw from the storehouse of Your love.

Lord, I look back through all of my experiences and see the ways that You have provided for my needs every day. You loved me when I was still a sinner, pardoned me by the blood of Jesus, and welcomed me as one of Your children. I thank You for all I have, especially the gift of my wife and children.

Father, I ask not for easier tasks but for better ability to meet the assignments You give me. Refresh me daily with Your strength and love, and give me the loving nature that can help ease the burdens of others.

SPEED

■ ■ ■

Father, one of the more dangerous sections of highway
near my home has been improved. The shoulders are
wider, some of the curves have been straightened, and
turning lanes have been added. Before the changes, driving errors could lead to disaster. But now, the likelihood
of accidents has been reduced. However, I drive faster on
the new section, speeding along where I used to drive with
more caution.

Lord, I am aware that You have made improvements
in my life. Thank You for taking care of the spiritual and
physical dangers as they occur along the road of my life.
I pray that I will not use the smoother path for speeding
along without paying attention to the many blessings You
have given me. I pray that I will never go faster than Your
guidance. Help me to direct my children to put their trust
in You, too. Only You can see the evil and temptations
that lie ahead waiting to wreck a life.

Keeping in Tune

"For my yoke is easy,
and my burden is light."
MATTHEW 11:30 NRSV

■ ■ ■

Father, while visiting a pioneer village with my children, we watched a blacksmith making horseshoes. First, he heated an iron bar until it was white-hot. Then he held it against an anvil with long pliers. With his other arm he swung the heavy hammer. To shape the horseshoe, he moved the iron bar but kept the hammer going at a steady pace, as if playing a tune. The blacksmith could work for hours because he let the hammer have its way.

Father, serving You becomes far less exhausting by being in tune with Your will. Weariness develops when I try to interpret Your will to meet my goals. Lord, help me grasp the advantages of keeping in tune with Your decrees, and help me teach this important concept to my children, as well. Many of our problems come from trying to bend Your will to our goals. Instead, help us work with You rather than against You.

ENCOURAGEMENT

CHEER

These things I have spoken unto you, that in me ye might
have peace. In the world ye shall have tribulation:
but be of good cheer; I have overcome the world.
JOHN 16:33 KJV

∎ ∎ ∎

Father, I watched the coach of my daughter's soccer team. He shouted encouragement at the top of his lungs. When a player missed a shot, he would later take them aside and explain in a gentle voice why they missed the play. Regardless of the score, he kept encouraging his players to do better—and they did. Like the coach, I have learned that encouragement improves performance, while criticism puts a damper on it.

Lord, I am thankful that Your Word is filled with encouragement. Even when You ask us to do the impossible, it becomes possible because we are not acting alone. You are with us, and You help and cheer us on to do better.

Father, at the soccer game, I saw young players scanning the stands looking for their fathers and mothers. When they saw their parents watching, they renewed their efforts. Thank You, Father, for always being with us, watching and encouraging.

Strength

*Therefore encourage one another and build
each other up, just as in fact you are doing.*
1 Thessalonians 5:11 niv

. . .

Father, I am continually amazed at the power of encouraging words. While hiking in the Grand Canyon, I saw a park ranger coming to the aid of a hiker who appeared to be totally exhausted. I assumed the individual would need to be airlifted out. Later, I met the park ranger and asked about the hiker. She explained that she had been able to "talk" him out. She suggested that he walk a little farther up the trail to a place with more shade. After a rest, she encouraged him, walked with him, and eventually he made it to the rim of the canyon.

Lord, I know that words are a powerful tool for strengthening people. The right words can build hope, restore confidence, and increase courage. Please give me the right words to inspire my children. Often, the only help I need to give them are words of encouragement.

Building Up

Humble yourselves therefore under the mighty hand of God, so that he may exalt you in due time. Cast all your anxiety on him, because he cares for you.
1 Peter 5:6–7 NRSV

■ ■ ■

Father, I used to sigh at the responsibilities that were imposed on me; now I rejoice that You strengthened me to meet the challenges. At one time I was entangled in the world; now I feel myself liberated by Your love. I used to feel embedded in sin; now I am living in Your affection. Before, I envied those who lived in better circumstances than myself; today, I recognize the blessings of my own prosperity. I feel that You have exalted me. You have raised me above grasping at the mundane so I can reach for greater achievements.

Father, in the same way that You have built my confidence, help me make it possible for my children to face the future with a positive attitude. I want them to go ahead with their plans, never giving undue concern that someone might be against them. Help them learn not to care about trivial distractions and instead concentrate on the vital goals that lead to happiness in a life of service to You.

SPOKEN LOVE

The tongue has the power of life and death,
and those who love it will eat its fruit.
PROVERBS 18:21 NIV

■ ■ ■

Lord, the Bible tells me of the power of Your words. You spoke the world into existence. You spoke a blessing to Abraham that eventually brought Your Son to Earth. Help me realize that my words are powerful, too, especially when addressing my children. I pray that I may never speak disparaging about them. But more importantly, I pray that I bless them with encouragement.

Father, sometimes I feel awkward trying to express my support for them in a meaningful way. Help me reinforce the power of my love and Your love by telling my children that they are special to me and to You. I pray that I'll be able to help them recognize and use the gifts You have given them. As they grow older, I pray for Your divine favor on their enterprises. May they always have faithful, loving, forgiving, and generous spirits.

ENDURANCE

STAMINA

Therefore, since we are surrounded by such a great cloud of witnesses, let us throw off everything that hinders and the sin that so easily entangles. And let us run with perseverance the race marked out for us.
HEBREWS 12:1 NIV

. . .

Father, I admire those individuals who show the endurance to complete difficult races that last for days. A great adventure takes long preparation, and sometimes people drop out even before the contest begins. Only a few make it to the starting line, and even fewer complete the race.

Lord, I think of the pioneers who crossed featureless deserts and climbed through heart-pounding mountain passes. They set out on the journey with the hope that a better life awaited them.

Father, help my family and me to realize that life is more like a marathon than a sprint. Give us the endurance to train for, enter, and complete the race. We need to wisely prepare for the race with all the equipment You have provided. In the Spirit, we will climb over mountain peaks, trek across desert valleys, and surmount other obstacles. And we are not alone; You are with us.

Thriving

I will praise thee, O Lord, with my whole heart; I will shew forth all thy marvellous works. I will be glad and rejoice in thee: I will sing praise to thy name, O thou most High.
Psalm 9:1–2 kjv

■ ■ ■

Dear Lord, during the early morning of a day I spent in the desert, insects crawled into the blossoms of a hedgehog cactus. At midday, a red-tailed hawk rested on a tall saguaro and watched for an incautious lizard to dart from its shade beneath a rock. Late in the evening, I observed a hungry coyote eating fruit that had dropped to the ground from a date palm.

Lord, I watched in fascination as life managed to survive and even thrive despite the harsh environment. I rejoiced in the wonder that I saw in Your created Earth. The plants and animals survived because they are Your special creation, and You equipped them with the traits they need for their life in the desert.

Father God, help me understand that You have equipped me with everything I need to live as Your child. May my family and I also survive and thrive in Your love.

STRIVING

This is a trustworthy saying that deserves full acceptance.
That is why we labor and strive, because we have put our
hope in the living God, who is the Savior of all people,
and especially of those who believe.
1 TIMOTHY 4:9–10 NIV

■ ■ ■

Father, spring is a time of growth and renewal, a time of new life and hope. This spring, an astonishing sight greeted me as I walked along a recently built walkway. A spring flower had managed to push through the hard asphalt. The delicate sprout had displayed unusual power as it shoved aside the heavy material that blocked its way to sunlight.

Lord, I am often surprised to see children who have managed to survive and even thrive despite the most difficult home life and adverse circumstances. Dedicated Christians have planted Your love in their hearts. These children show the amazing resilience of those who strive to reach Your love. I pray that I give to my children the desire to always reach toward You.

Father, I want to daily renew myself spiritually. I pray that I will manifest strength of character to overcome those forces that get in my way of growing in Your light.

PATIENCE

Therefore, as God's chosen people, holy and
dearly loved, clothe yourselves with compassion,
kindness, humility, gentleness and patience.
COLOSSIANS 3:12 NIV

■ ■ ■

Dear Father, impatience is one of my faults. I am intolerant of delay at work, irritated when family members do not share my urgency, and restless in the face of inaction. Patience is an attribute that I need in double measure as a father. I need the patience for everyday delays as well as long-term patience as my children develop the maturity to make intelligent decisions.

Lord, I also need to learn patience with You. Sometimes I impatiently decide You are not going to solve a problem, and I act outside Your will. I make ill-considered decisions and take reckless actions that endanger me physically and spiritually.

Father, I trust in You. I pray that Your inner peace will sustain me. My goal is neither the impatience of rash actions nor the inaction of passive resignation but the endurance of a mature Christian who perseveres while awaiting Your will.

FAMILY

Values

I pray that the God of our Lord Jesus Christ,
the Father of glory, may give you a spirit of wisdom
and revelation as you come to know him.
EPHESIANS 1:17 NRSV

■ ■ ■

Father, I hear the word family used in a variety of ways today. Television has the family hour, which is for family-oriented shows, although they often are not. Some families designate a space in their home as a family room but seldom use it except for watching television. The term family man may merely mean a man who has a wife and children.

Lord, I pray that I live up to the term family man to the full extent of its meaning. I pray that under Your leadership, I will build a strong family on the rock of Your wisdom.

Father, may my family and I develop shared Christian goals and spiritual values. May we have a long-term commitment to one another and to You. After my children become adults, may they still reside under the tent of Your blessings.

ILLUMINATE

But you, beloved, are not in darkness, for that day to
surprise you like a thief; for you are all children of light and
children of the day; we are not of the night or of darkness.
1 THESSALONIANS 5:4–5 NRSV

■ ■ ■

Lord, the other night during a power failure, I was the first to find a flashlight. The little light was enough to dispel the darkness. Because I carried the light, members of my family gathered around me.

Father, I recognize one of my roles is to be a light to my children. I need to illuminate the proper choices in their lives—the righteous choices. I must be firm, with a resolute will, yet not overbearing.

Lord, Your radiance illuminates all creation, yet I see people stumbling in spiritual gloom. Although I am but a pale reflection of Your brilliance, I pray that the teaching I do becomes a beacon that draws lost souls into the circle of Your light. May my light never dazzle but reveal. Guide me so that I push out the darkness and fill the lives of others with the light of Christ.

PRECIOUS

For he says, "At an acceptable time I have listened to you,
and on a day of salvation I have helped you." See, now is
the acceptable time; see, now is the day of salvation!
2 CORINTHIANS 6:2 NRSV

■ ■ ■

Father, I am fascinated by time-travel stories. Going back
to re-experience a pleasant event or to correct a decision that led to disaster is an idea that I find attractive.
Of course, it is impossible to go back in time and undo
events. Time is a one-way street.

Lord, Your Word begins with a mention of time, "In
the beginning," and ends with a mention of time, "Surely I
am coming soon." I see my journey on Earth as aboard a
time machine that can only move forward. I must give my
best efforts the first time.

Father, I wish to use well the time You have given me.
I must wisely decide what is the best use of my time. But
help me recognize that time is too precious to waste pur-
suing what many in the world think of as success. Instead,
direct me to invest my time to develop closer harmony with
my family and with You.

School

A wise man will hear, and will increase learning; and a man of understanding shall attain unto wise counsels.
Proverbs 1:5 kjv

■ ■ ■

Heavenly Father, as part of my duties as a parent, I deal with the schools that my children attend. In many instances, the procedures and policies seem to require a considerable capacity for patience. Please equip me with that patience and with the insight to help improve the education of my children and other students, as well.

I pray that our educators have the ability to motivate children to their best achievement. Provide our teachers with the means to instill in students a joy for learning and the capacity for a lifetime of seeking the truth. Develop in our teachers and students boldness to express their love for You.

Revive our education system so teachers and students can express their Christian beliefs. May teachers be able to show the religious context that guided the founding of our great nation. May teachers be a role model of excellence and integrity.

GOALS OF A FATHER

*For you know that we dealt with each of you as
a father deals with his own children, encouraging,
comforting and urging you to live lives worthy of God,
who calls you into his kingdom and glory.*
1 THESSALONIANS 2:11–12 NIV

. . .

Heavenly Father, I am perplexed by how the world sees fathers. In the old television shows, the man of the house was a wise, successful, and morally superior man. Today, the father is often portrayed as a bewildered but loveable buffoon without the foggiest notion of how to solve the problems his children face.

Lord, as a father I want to provide affection and emotional support. Help me communicate in a way that they can understand. May I give training in proper behavior and supply a gentle but constant pressure for them to develop to their highest capabilities. Help my children understand that my success in training them requires responsibilities on their part, too.

As my children grow, I want them to gain the wisdom to remember and emulate the good things that they saw in my life. Even when my children are not present, I desire that my actions be those of a godly father. Most important of all, I want to be the cornerstone of a righteous family.

OPEN LINE

Listen, children, to a father's instruction,
and be attentive, that you may gain insight; for I
give you good precepts: do not forsake my teaching.
PROVERBS 4:1–2 NRSV

■ ■ ■

If my children are away on Mother's Day they call their mother, and on Father's Day they call me, too—collect. If they are home on Mother's Day, they take us out to eat, and I pay. On Father's Day they take us out to eat, too—and I pay. But I do get to enjoy conversation with my children.

Lord, help me make it plain to my children that they have an open line of communication to me and that I will be there in time of crisis. I pray they also realize that I will listen when they simply wish to pass the time of day.

Father God, I think of the times that I have put in collect calls to You. I know You are happy to receive my prayers, regardless of the circumstances. I pray that I will be an example of a loving, patient father like You.

CHECKLIST

He hath shewed thee, O man, what is good;
and what doth the LORD require of thee, but to do justly,
and to love mercy, and to walk humbly with thy God?
MICAH 6:8 KJV

. . .

Father, my company is big on checklists. I must go through a sequence of steps before I can start a complex piece of equipment. Sometimes I am surprised at what I find: a fuel gauge that reads inaccurately, a switch left on by the previous operator, a stuck valve, or a safety shield that is missing.

Lord, I pray that I will take my duties as a father as seriously as I do when working around heavy equipment. Help me constantly examine what is required of me to avoid physical or spiritual injury to those under my care. I will teach honesty by keeping promises that I make to my family. I will exercise courage when others try to intimidate me. I will show justice by being fair with everyone. I will demonstrate respect by treating my family with love and deference. I will model obedience by reading and following Your teachings.

SEASONS OF LIFE

There is a time for everything, and a
season for every activity under the heavens:
a time to be born and a time to die.
ECCLESIASTES 3:1–2 NIV

■ ■ ■

Father, each year as I watch the seasons unfold, I become more aware of the changes in my life. I see the growth of spring foliage, the nearly imperceptible change in the larger trees from year to year, then the appearance of fall colors. Later in the year when I find frost on my windshield, I become aware that the growing season has ended and that cold weather will soon grip the land.

Lord, as the years have slipped away, I realize that my children are in their final preparations to leave home. I sometimes resist the changes that their greater maturity brings. But change is a part of Your design. You created the seasons for healthy growth, and change must take place in my family, too.

Heavenly Father, it is time for my children to seek their own way. I pray that the way they seek and the path they find is in keeping with Your will.

FELLOWSHIP

UNITY

And the glory which thou gavest me I have given them;
that they may be one, even as we are one.
JOHN 17:22 KJV

■ ■ ■

Righteous Father, I am humbled when I realize that Jesus, on the night He was betrayed, prayed for unity of believers. I look at Your Word through different eyes than other Christians and often cannot fully agree with them. But help me focus on our many vital common beliefs rather than our few trivial differences. Help me see the strength in unity and the danger in discord.

Lord, thank You for giving my family the blessing of fellowship with believers. In our unity with others, we are strengthened. Our joy is renewed, and we grow in knowledge and understanding of Your will.

Father, often it is easy to agree if the agreement is to do nothing. Let my agreement be to act and do, not to sit back and wait. Let me join the fellowship of believers so we become a force for righteousness—Jesus would want it.

Forward

So we fix our eyes not on what is seen,
but on what is unseen, since what is seen is
temporary, but what is unseen is eternal.
2 Corinthians 4:18 NIV

∎ ∎ ∎

Father, as my daughter completed her driving training course, she reported that the best advice she received was to look ahead in the distance. The car took a straighter course, and she could control it better if she looked where it was going, not where it was.

Lord, I recall the words of Leroy "Satchel" Paige: "Don't look back. Something may be gaining on you." This principle is useful in my life. In my day-to-day living, circumstances often seem to engulf me. But if I look at the point where I intend to go, not at my present position, it becomes clearer what I should do.

Father, I know that it is impossible to know what the future holds. I cannot direct my own way. That is the reason that I must depend on You. I pray that I will center my objectives on being in fellowship with You.

BELIEVERS

*Not giving up meeting together, as some are in
the habit of doing, but encouraging one another—
and all the more as you see the Day approaching.*
HEBREWS 10:25 NIV

■ ■ ■

Heavenly Father, reading the Bible, talking to You in
prayer, singing hymns, and meeting with other Christians
help fortify my spiritual life. Only by becoming strong in
You can I overcome obstacles. I need to assemble with
other Christians because I gain strength by associating
with those who love You.

Lord, help my children feel blessed to have the opportunity to gather with other Christians. Singing, praying,
and studying Your Word will inspire them to a closer walk
with You. May they always be glad to participate with
other believers in strengthening one another and in wor-
shipping You.

Father, I, too, need the fellowship of dedicated believers. I pray that I lead my entire family to take advantage
of every opportunity to attend church services. May we
worship and glorify You. Help me realize that we are
blessed through fellowship with others.

CAMARADERIE

Therefore, as God's chosen people, holy and dearly loved,
clothe yourselves with compassion, kindness, humility,
gentleness and patience. Bear with each other and forgive
one another if any of you has a grievance against someone.
Forgive as the Lord forgave you. And over all these virtues
put on love, which binds them all together in perfect unity.
COLOSSIANS 3:12–14 NIV

■ ■ ■

Father, I have heard fellowship described as "fellows in the same ship." They willingly work together because the success of their voyage depends upon mutual trust and a feeling of kinship.

Lord, my family and I are working with other Christians toward common goals of living justly, walking humbly, and loving mercy. Because all Christians share these goals, help me recognize a common fellowship.

Father, help me embrace all Christians as my brothers and sisters because we have an underlying oneness with You. We share the same faith and the same hope. Create a desire in me to embrace them with love and kinship. We are truly fellows in the same ship.

Anger

Those with good sense are slow to anger,
and it is their glory to overlook an offense.
Proverbs 19:11 NRSV

. . .

Father, my children can be an object lesson in how I should deal with my anger. I notice that a child's anger is short lived. Two little friends can have a disagreement, and within a brief time they are playing together again.

Lord, I realize that anger and forgiveness cannot exist together. Only after I rid myself of my anger can I begin the process of forgiveness. Anger and a peaceful mind are mutually exclusive, too, because I cannot have a loving and calm mind when resentment is present. Anger not only keeps me from feeling love for the target of my hostility, but it prevents me from loving others, as well. When I rage against another person, everything else is pushed aside.

Father, I pray that I learn not only to control my anger but also how to diffuse it and rid my mind of it. May I be an example for my family by putting anger in its place.

REMOVE

As far as the east is from the west, so far hath he removed our transgressions from us. Like as a father pitieth his children, so the LORD pitieth them that fear him.
PSALM 103:12–13 KJV

■ ■ ■

Father, I am always making mistakes. As a child, I used an eraser to rub out the errors and correct them, although the erasures were obvious on the paper. More recently, I used touch-up paint to cover scratches on door frames, but getting the paints to match exactly was impossible. Errors can never be completely concealed.

Lord, I often see how my children try to hide a problem. What they claimed was a clean bedroom often had trash stowed under the bed. Once, they glued a broken vase back together to pass as undamaged, but the repair failed to fool anyone.

Father, I sometimes make bad judgments and sin against You. Within my own power, I cannot correct them, but I trust in Jesus to blot out all iniquities. When You remove them, You don't leave a smudgy erasure or a mismatched touch-up. Thank You for removing them entirely so they no longer exist.

Injustices

*"Whenever you stand praying, forgive, if you have
anything against anyone; so that your Father in
heaven may also forgive you your trespasses."*
MARK 11:25 NRSV

■ ■ ■

Sometimes, Lord, my mind wanders back to my earlier
life. For some reason, injustices immediately come to mind
more readily than pleasant experiences. Anger surfaces
when I dwell on the unfair treatment I have experienced.
I had many privileged opportunities and blessings, but I
remember the negative events with far more emotion than
the positive occasions.

Father, I recall a saying that I saw on a sundial:
"I count only the sunny hours." I see this attitude in my
young children who quickly replace the howls of being
slighted with songs of happiness. Help me develop an attitude that focuses on my blessings.

Forgiving Lord, help me press on with my life. Review-
ing reruns of my past serves no purpose. I shall not use
past events as an excuse for my current shortcomings.
With Your help, I will release the resentments I have carried so long and accept responsibility for my own actions.

UNCONDITIONAL

"My offenses will be sealed up in a bag;
you will cover over my sin."
JOB 14:17 NIV

■ ■ ■

Father, my life is often in shambles because I fail to follow Your good guidance. I ask Your forgiveness. Thank You for the gift of Your Son who, through His sacrifice, gives reconciliation and mercy. Continue to deal gently with me.

Lord, I participate in Your forgiveness through my forgiveness of others. There is no limit to Your forgiveness of me, so there should be no limit to my forgiveness of others. Grant me the ability to renounce anger and resentment against those who have hurt me. I know it is impossible for me to do this on my own, but through You I have the ability to do the impossible. You excuse my faults without demanding punishment. Give me the grace to do the same for others.

Father, I pardon to the extent that I love, and I love my children dearly. Let them see the extent of my love through my forgiveness.

GUARDIAN

Before and After

Even before a word is on my tongue, O Lord,
you know it completely. You hem me in, behind
and before, and lay your hand upon me.
Psalm 139:4–5 NRSV

■ ■ ■

Father, when my daughter began to crawl, her mother and I were always there, picking up what she had dropped and setting straight what she turned over. But we also went before her, making sure she could not pull something down on herself. We put away those items too dangerous to be in her hands. We prepared a safe play area for her.

Lord, as my daughter grew older, we gave her help without her being aware of it. A little child who leaves toys strewn around needs our help in putting them away. An older child leaves a series of events that needs straightened out, too. Just as importantly as when she was smaller, we still took steps to smooth the way in advance of her.

Father, I realize now that You are both behind and ahead of me. You not only clean up my mistakes, You also level the path before me. Thank You, Father, for doing all for me, both seen and unseen.

SURVIVAL

Nevertheless I am continually with you; you hold
my right hand. You guide me with your counsel,
and afterward you will receive me with honor.
PSALM 73:23–24 NRSV

■ ■ ■

Father, whenever I take my family hiking, I feel more comfortable if I carry a trail guide. But sometimes I put it in my pocket and forget to check the landmarks as we pass them. When the trail divides and I reach a point of decision, I regret that I have not traced my progress more carefully. I not only need to carry a trail guide, I also need to study it as I go.

Heavenly Father, Your Word is my survival guide. When a crisis arises, I turn to the Bible for comfort. But when my study has been lax, I feel like I am on the trail with an inadequately used trail guide. It would have been better to develop the comfort of Your Word before the emergency arose.

Lord, I want to equip my children with the survival traits to avoid having the world overcome them. Help them remember to carry Your trail guide—the Bible—and also read it and make it their guide in all spiritual matters.

DECISIONS

Let your speech always be gracious, seasoned with salt,
so that you may know how you ought to answer everyone.
COLOSSIANS 4:6 NRSV

■ ■ ■

Lord, I often must make decisions that affect others on
short notice. Despite complex situations, I must answer
"yes" or "no" and do it quickly. The proper course of action is not always obvious because I lack all the facts necessary to make a well-informed choice. Yet I cannot delay
because the decision must be made today, not tomorrow.

Father, sometimes my children come to me asking for
permission to do some activity. Help me take the time to
be better informed about how my decision may affect them.
Often, the question arises when other matters distract me.
Please help me put my family first, so that my thinking is
in focus.

Dear Jesus, I always want my choices to be in keeping with the examples set by You. But when the options
appear equally valid, each having risks and benefits, I
pray I will be both wise and decisive.

PERSPECTIVE

*"For the eyes of the Lord are on the righteous,
and his ears are open to their prayer."*
1 PETER 3:12 NRSV

■ ■ ■

Dear Lord, viewing the world from a thousand feet up in a hot air balloon gives me an unusual perspective. I can see dangerous situations develop before they become obvious to others. I can see that the canoe in the stream will hit rapids around the bend. I can see two cars coming toward one another along a country lane, but because of a hill, the drivers can't see each other. My eyes are no sharper than theirs, but I have a better perspective.

Father, I know You have a better viewpoint. You can see into hearts, and You know what the future holds. You can see situations before they arise in our lives and prepare us for the proper way for us to have a victory over them. Please continue to watch over us. I pray that through the study of Your Word and our prayers for Your guidance, we will be lifted to a better vantage point and will plan our lives according to Your direction.

BEACON

*"The people who sat in darkness have seen a
great light, and for those who sat in the region
and shadow of death light has dawned."*
MATTHEW 4:16 NRSV

■ ■ ■

Father, while traveling in the desert country of the south-
west, I noticed that some of the older ranches had a tall
pole with a lantern on top. I learned that this custom had
begun years ago. People would ride away from the ranch
during the day and find themselves confused as to the
way back after sunset. On a dark, moonless night the
landmarks disappeared. They could only find their way
back to the safety of the ranch by looking for the beacon.

Lord, although only a pinprick of light in a vast ex-
panse of darkness, the tiny lantern guided the way for the
lost travelers. Sometimes one must show the way by active
leading. But the beacon guided others merely by letting
its light shine at the right place.

Father, I pray that I serve as a beacon for my family. I
pray that by recognizing me as a source of guidance, they
will find the way to You as the shelter for their lives.

LISTEN

My dear brothers and sisters, take note of this:
Everyone should be quick to listen,
slow to speak and slow to become angry.
JAMES 1:19 NIV

■ ■ ■

Lord, I study to improve my skills as a father. Sometimes this training merely makes me feel bad because after learning what I should do, I realize that I fall far short of perfection. For example, to communicate well, I should first listen and give my full attention to the speaker. I should strive to fully understand what they are telling me, repeat what they say in my own words, and ask questions. But rather than listening, I often merely exercise patience while waiting for my children to finish so that I can talk. How hard it is to ask questions rather than to give answers!

Father, although I think I know the right answer and can compel my children to agree with me, it is better to communicate in such a way that they choose the best path.

Lord, also help me use listening skills when I come before You. Give me the patience to wait for Your message. May I tune in to You with my mind and heart.

Intersection

How much better to get wisdom than gold, to get insight rather than silver! The highway of the upright avoids evil; those who guard their ways preserve their lives.
PROVERBS 16:16–17 NIV

■ ■ ■

Father, my life has defining moments. At these intersections, I am presented with choices that will forever affect my family and me. Some intersections are merely different paths to the same destination. But others are clearly choices that take a measure of my character. To be a wholesome example to my children, I must choose righteousness over convenience.

Lord, You have the ability to make even my bad choices work out for me. Any incorrect decision can be righted if I will call upon Your name and repent. But I know, too, that the effect of a wrong choice can linger. It is far better to have the Christian principles and strength to make the right decision in the first place.

Father, You are at all of the intersections of my life. You are there to show me the right way to go. I pray that I'll recognize Your heavenly guidance and have the commitment to follow the correct path.

TRUE COURSE

*Ye did run well; who did hinder you
that ye should not obey the truth?*
GALATIANS 5:7 KJV

∎ ∎ ∎

Dear Lord, when I am hiking with my children, I am constantly checking my direction with a compass and a trail guide. The little ones depend on me to set the right course for them. As a compass is drawn to the poles, so I am drawn to You, knowing that others follow in my steps.

Heavenly Father, my soul seeks to align in the true direction with Your mercy and grace. You, O Lord, are my righteous Creator. I pray that I will live a consecrated life through Your enabling power. Please guide me to live rightly and dispel the negative powers that could draw me off course.

Father, I pray that I will convey to my children a determination to follow the heavenly compass. May they be drawn to Your path and not depart from it.

HAPPINESS

GRATITUDE

Is anyone among you in trouble? Let them pray.
Is anyone happy? Let them sing songs of praise.
JAMES 5:13 NIV

■ ■ ■

Father, during a conference break, I returned to my hotel room to use the time to work on a report. As I approached, I heard singing in the room. I walked closer and discovered the maid happily doing her chores. She was singing in happiness. I listened for a moment in secret admiration and then backed away rather than disturb her.

Lord, the young woman's happiness didn't depend upon her economic condition or station in life. The song she was singing was a Christian hymn that told the source of her joy—You. Her happiness flowed naturally from the gratitude of knowing that You cared about her.

Father, I had approached the room feeling harried and stressed. But the woman showed me how to complete my day filled with gratitude and happiness. Instead of working on the report, I telephoned home and left a message assuring my children that I would be home that night in time to tuck them into bed.

MEMORIES

*I will remember the deeds of the L*ORD*; yes,*
I will remember your miracles of long ago. I will consider
all your works and meditate on all your mighty deeds.
PSALM 77:11–12 NIV

■ ■ ■

Lord, I've heard people who recount the events in their
lives by jumping from one crisis to another. In between
misfortunes, they may have experienced periods of calm
or even happiness. But to them, those times are merely
blank pages in their memory because they only remember
those times when they were miserable.

Father, I pray that I will remember the blessings, not
the trials, and enjoy happiness, not wallow in the times of
distress. I recognize that happiness is not increased by
material wealth nor destroyed by physical trials. Instead,
it grows in proportion to how willing I am to center my
heart on considering Your blessings.

Lord, I am most happy when I clearly identify what
You want me to do, and I go about doing it with all my
strength. Happiness as a father is leading my family in
Your way and working vigorously to earn their respect
and love.

REIGN

*"And now, my children, listen to me: happy are
those who keep my ways. Hear instruction
and be wise, and do not neglect it."*
PROVERBS 8:32–33 NRSV

∎ ∎ ∎

Father, I sit alone in the dim early morning light to reflect
on the happiness I am feeling. I'm living a full and inter-
esting life. I'm raising a family, luxuriating in the company
of friends, and working at a job that I enjoy. As I spend
time in meditation, feelings of gratitude and happiness
flood over me. You have been so good to me!

Lord, I recognize You as the source of all that I possess. I express my admiration to You, the Creator, whose
hand I see so clearly in every aspect of my life.

Father, may I continue to have an uninterrupted
pursuit for the happiness that comes from You. I see how
happy people are who put Your will before their own. I
can be truly happy only as a person who yields to You.
Help me reach that happy state where You reign supreme
in my life.

CHEERFUL

*I know that there is nothing better for people
than to be happy and to do good while they live.
That each of them may eat and drink, and find
satisfaction in all their toil—this is the gift of God.*
ECCLESIASTES 3:12–13 NIV

■ ■ ■

Father, my daily life is made easier by the work of other people. I wear clothes made by strangers, some of whom live half a world away. I eat food grown on distant shores or caught in faraway oceans. I ride in vehicles assembled by hands unknown to me. I have enjoyed the labors of others.

Lord, I want to show gratitude to those who do things for me and thank those who provide personal service. Yet I see that even without personal contact, people that I have never met make my life better. I am grateful for their efforts but cannot directly repay them. But I can express my gratitude to You and show happiness to others. I can maintain an optimistic outlook and be kind and cheerful. May I increase the pool of goodwill around me by my happiness and gratitude. Help me instill in my children the spiritual fruit of joy.

SERENITY

*"Can any one of you by worrying
add a single hour to your life?"*
MATTHEW 6:27 NIV

■ ■ ■

Father, thanks for calming my agitation in times of distress. With Your peace, I smile at my past foolish concerns. Some situations had already passed and could not be changed, others were unlikely to have happened, and some were trivial and not worth my emotional energy. But worry gave a small concern a long shadow. Through my actions, I could have changed only a few of the situations that troubled me.

Lord, plant me in faith, hope, and love. Shower on me the blessings that saturate my heart so thoroughly that I have room only for sensible concerns—those over which I can make a difference. I pray that I will see my troubles more clearly in Your wisdom.

Father, help me develop the serenity that produces a calming influence on others, especially the members of my family. By trusting in Your guidance, we can overcome any crisis.

CHANGE

For the grace of God. . .teaches us to say "No"
to ungodliness and worldly passions, and to live self-
controlled, upright and godly lives in this present age,
while we wait for the blessed hope—the appearing of
the glory of our great God and Savior, Jesus Christ.
TITUS 2:11–13 NIV

• • •

Father, I tear pages from my desk calendar and see how quickly time is getting away from me. My life is in a headlong rush into a future filled with changes. I appreciate that in these changing times, You do not change. You eliminate the dread of change and fill me with hope so that I can look forward with confidence.

Lord, I pray that I develop the trust in You that brings stability to my family. Grow in us the faith to see that no matter how things turn out, problems that tax us today will be for our best in Your eternal plan. May we look beyond the dark events of today to the bright future of a home with You.

Father, I do not know what changes will overtake me in the future, but I know that You can take care of the things that concern me today and protect me from what comes against me tomorrow. You bring hope to me.

Never Without

I trust in you; do not let me be put to shame,
nor let my enemies triumph over me. No one
who hopes in you will ever be put to shame.
PSALM 25:2–3 NIV

· · ·

Father, sometimes I can see that my children have become despondent. Their outlook becomes gloomy. It is as if some of the light has gone out in their lives. Yet such a feeling is only justified if they are without hope. That certainly is not the case. Those who place their trust in You should never lose hope. Guide me in helping my teenage children learn ways to overcome negative emotions.

Lord, I, too, can have a troubled mind. However, I know that Your love, the grace of Jesus Christ, and the guidance of the Holy Spirit are with me. Help me face the challenges before me with boldness. Give me strength to shake off anything that troubles my mind so that I press on each day with a clear purpose. Help me ignore those troubling concerns that might slow my steps.

CRISIS

■ ■ ■

Lord, sometimes when a crisis comes my way, I am un-
daunted because I have faced the same problem before
and think I can handle it. But should the crisis be in an
area of which I have no experience or ability, then I am
plunged into despair. Most troubling are unexpected
medical emergencies that strike my family. I am presented
with a situation that is beyond my ability to make better.
In my helplessness, I imagine the most ominous outcome.
I can't think; I can't eat; I walk around as one in a daze.

Father, You are my greatest resource when a crisis
strikes. I must remember that I can call upon You. Help
me trust in You to carry me through the adversity. Comfort
and encourage me during these difficult times. Should I
ever fall into a period of depression and find it difficult to
feel optimistic about the future, lift me up and let me see
the bright glow of Your love.

LISTENING

GUIDE

By day the Lord commands his steadfast love, and at
night his song is with me, a prayer to the God of my life.
PSALM 42:8 NRSV

. . .

Father, I once had a supervisor who had an open-door policy. Whenever I was torn about the best course of action for solving a problem, I would spend a few minutes talking with him. Sometimes he suggested a choice I should take or cautioned me against an option I had proposed.

Lord, I pray that my children recognize that I am willing to talk about their problems. Let them come to me so I can offer guidance. Grant me the ability to provide sensible suggestions and to correctly identify what they should do based on Your unfailing wisdom.

Father, I am thankful that You have an open-door policy. I can talk to You day or night about the things that are troubling me. It is a comfort to know that You are there to listen. I know that You will make clear to me the correct decision.

URGENT

*Then people brought little children to Jesus for
him to place his hands on them and pray for them.
But the disciples rebuked them. Jesus said, "Let the
little children come to me, and do not hinder them,
for the kingdom of heaven belongs to such as these."*
MATTHEW 19:13–14 NIV

■ ■ ■

Father, during my busy schedule, I can see unimportant items as urgent while vital ones are shoved to the back of my mind. Answering a ringing telephone may seem urgent, but listening to my daughter tell about her day at school may be more important.

Lord, thank You for Your example of how to identify the proper choices. You encouraged little children to spend time with You. You devoted Your time to those others would have ignored.

Father, help me reschedule my time to put the important things first. The time that I spend with You and my family should take precedence over urgent matters that become meaningless after the deadline has passed.

KNOCK

"Here I am! I stand at the door and knock.
If anyone hears my voice and opens the door,
I will come in and eat with that person, and they with me."
REVELATION 3:20 NIV

■ ■ ■

Father, sometimes distractions can derail my train of thought. When doing paperwork at home that requires my full attention, I used to lock the door to my office so my children would not come rushing in with the latest stories of school or events on the playing field. They knocked and waited—sometimes with more patience than I thought they were capable of—until I found a stopping place and opened the door.

Once, I came by and saw my boy sitting down outside the door. The door had been closed, and he thought I was inside. He had knocked, but when he heard no answer, he sat down by the door and waited for me to come out. Now I've decided to delay work that requires quiet time until after my children go to sleep.

Father, sometimes I close the door to You, and You knock and knock in vain at my heart. But now I've decided to keep an open door to my children and to You.

FRIENDS

"Is there anyone among you who, if your child asks for bread, will give a stone? Or if the child asks for a fish, will give a snake? If you then, who are evil, know how to give good gifts to your children, how much more will your Father in heaven give good things to those who ask him!"
MATTHEW 7:9–11 NRSV

◼ ◼ ◼

Father, when I meet a friend, I take the time to ask about his day and talk with him. When he is visiting me at home, I make him comfortable, offer refreshments, and discuss subjects of interest to him. Should he have a task that needs done, I am willing to offer a helping hand. My best friend is a person who I know and trust. I know his faults, and he knows mine, but we ignore them anyway. We view one another in the best light.

Lord, I am aware that I am often more considerate of my friends than I am of members of my own family. When I seek to please everyone else at the expense of my family, I know the emphasis is in the wrong place. I should rather gain the good opinion of my family than impress any friend. Help me to treat my family with respect, dignity, and consideration.

EMULATE

*Show yourself in all respects a model of good works,
and in your teaching show integrity, gravity, and sound
speech that cannot be censured; then any opponent will
be put to shame, having nothing evil to say of us.*
TITUS 2:7–8 NRSV

■ ■ ■

Lord, I know that for my young children, I am a role model of You. How I treat them will shape how they will perceive You as they grow older. Will they see You as fair, affectionate, compassionate, and patient? Or will they see a father as unreasonable, aloof, callous, and impatient? Will they view You as One who provides for their needs and understands their fears? Or will they see a father as neglectful and uncaring?

Father, I want my children to approach me as one who will help. I do not want them to mistrust me. If their childhood is poisoned by fear, they may find it more difficult to approach You. If they are suspicious of my goodness, they may be unable to clearly see Your goodness. Father, I cannot perfectly emulate You, but I pray that my children see enough of You in me that they grow into an understanding of Your true, loving nature.

Appreciate

Know therefore that the LORD thy God,
he is God, the faithful God, which keepeth covenant
and mercy with them that love him and keep his
commandments to a thousand generations.
DEUTERONOMY 7:9 KJV

...

Omnipotent Father, there are no limitations to the amount of love and attention You can individually bestow upon each of Your children. Although I receive Your rich blessings all the time, day and night, I pray that I do not take Your love for granted.

Lord, the more I know You and understand You, the more I see and appreciate Your love. I pray that I will experience You more deeply so that my love for You will increase. You have taught me that sacrifices must be made for love to grow. I submit to You. Demolish me and then rebuild me so I may be one with You.

Father, my children are often not fully aware of the many measures I take to improve their lives. Although they know they are loved, the depth of that love is difficult for them to comprehend.

Lord, I realize that Your love extends beyond anything I can comprehend.

ACTIVE

*And so we know and rely on the love God
has for us. God is love. Whoever lives in
love lives in God, and God in them.*
1 JOHN 4:16 NIV

■ ■ ■

Lord, I've seen parents who love a child deeply, but it is
not entirely clear that the child returns that love to any
depth. The lack of reciprocated love is devastating for the
parents and disastrous for the child. I pray that I am not
like one of those children who fails to see the love that You
lavish upon me.

Father, I read that You are love. Although *love* is a
small word, it stands for a concept that is too great for me
to completely wrap my limited mind around. In Your goodness, You created the universe and everything in it as a
place to show Your love. Develop in me the willingness to
act according to Your will, not because of Your commands
but because of my love for You.

Heavenly Father, I want to love You, my wife, my children, and my neighbors. Help me go beyond the emotion
of love to the action of love.

REUNION

But if we walk in the light, as he is in the light,
we have fellowship with one another, and the blood
of Jesus, his Son, purifies us from all sin.
1 JOHN 1:7 NIV

■ ■ ■

Father, winter holiday seasons are a time for family re-unions. Now that my children are grown, married, and have children, this is my favorite time of year. Warmth radiates from hugs, smiles, and love. Grandchildren bring gifts that they have made with their own hands, and we cherish these gifts because of their special efforts.

Lord, despite our family being separated for most of the year, we hold one another in enormous respect and affection. Some people may wonder how a family that lives so far from one another can be so close. It is because we have learned the blessings of putting our lives in Your hands. All the prayers, correction, and training that my wife and I heaped on our children when they were little have now reaped the benefit of lives living in harmony with You and fellowship with one another. Thank You for giving me this loving family.

MORALITY

Armor

Finally, be strong in the Lord and in his mighty power.
Put on the full armor of God.
Ephesians 6:10–11 NIV

■ ■ ■

Father, when I pack for a long vacation with my family, I double-check my list to be certain that we have not left anything behind. During our travels, I always take a head count before we leave a location so that no one is missing. Even the best of families can have a frightening and embarrassing situation of a child left behind.

Lord, I am also taking my family on a spiritual journey. It is important that I help them pack for that trip, as well. I need to equip them with Your armor—truth, righteousness, the good news of Jesus, faith, salvation, and the sword of the Spirit.

Father, I often become too concerned with the mundane aspects of my children's lives—clothes, sports, money, and school. I pray that I go beyond my checklists of everyday matters to the more important spiritual subjects. I pray that they are traveling with You as we journey along the road of life.

PEER PRESSURE

My child, keep your father's commandment, and do not forsake your mother's teaching. Bind them upon your heart always; tie them around your neck. When you walk, they will lead you; when you lie down, they will watch over you; and when you awake, they will talk with you.
PROVERBS 6:20–22 NRSV

■ ■ ■

Heavenly Father, as my children become older, they become subject to greater peer pressure that can lead to harmful dependencies, destructive relationships, and risky behaviors. They feel pressure in countless ways—from their choices in clothing and music, to the dangers of drugs, alcohol, and immorality.

Lord, I do want to give them the freedom to make the ordinary choices of daily life. The more they trust themselves and their ability to make independent decisions, the more likely they'll be able to withstand the undue influence of peer pressure.

When my children face big decisions, give me the confidence to teach the principles from the Bible that have stood the test of time. Remind me to always be ready to give guidance based on Your Word.

Serve God

*Now therefore put away, said he, the strange gods which
are among you, and incline your heart unto the LORD God
of Israel. And the people said unto Joshua, The LORD
our God will we serve, and his voice will we obey.*
JOSHUA 24: 23–24 KJV

■ ■ ■

Father, help me be mindful that I represent You to those I
meet each day. I cannot place my Christian service in one
compartment and my secular duties in another. I recall
a decision faced by a friend, a real estate salesman. His
supervisor told him, "Tell the truth as long as you can and
then start selling." He chose to leave that employer rather
than compromise his Christian principles. I admire him,
and I pray that I will also be willing to suffer loss rather
than discredit You.

Lord, I know that some people enjoy their jobs. Others work because they enjoy what their wages will enable
them to do. But I've seen people in jobs that test their ability to remain faithful. I would not want my children to fall
into such a difficult situation. I pray that through prayer
and study, they will find occupations that suit their skills,
interest, and abilities. Help them put being Your servants
as the chief goal of their résumés.

VOTE

If my people, which are called by my name,
shall humble themselves, and pray, and seek my face,
and turn from their wicked ways; then will I hear from
heaven, and will forgive their sin, and will heal their land.
2 CHRONICLES 7:14 KJV

■ ■ ■

Father, at each election, I cast my ballot and wear the sticker that says, "I voted." When I think about my Christian service, I realize that my most influential vote is the way that I live. Each day I make choices—the products I buy, the programs I decide to view while surfing television channels, and my willingness to participate in church activities. I vote by my attitudes and actions.

Lord, my young children may have only a slight recognition of who I voted for in an election, but every day they see if I am a moral leader and a sincere Christian. Direct me in showing them that the most important vote is how I live my life.

I pray I will vote for justice, honesty, and moral responsibility, not only at the ballot box, but also in the daily choices that I make. I want my spiritual influence to have a positive effect on my family and community.

COUNTERFEIT

But lay up for yourselves treasures in heaven,
where neither moth nor rust doth corrupt,
and where thieves do not break through nor steal.
MATTHEW 6:20 KJV

■ ■ ■

Lord, choices come to me in pairs. Do I desire power or respect, wealth or grace, status or Your glory? Which is more important to me—worldly honor or everlasting glory, a long life on Earth or an eternal life with You? Ambition may blind me to seek a choice that will lead me away from a life of service to You.

Father, when I think about power, wealth, or status, I must ask myself where my treasures lie. Help me reject the counterfeit goals as nothing to be esteemed. I want to reject the wrong choices to make room for the right ones. May I have a genuine determination to bring Your Word into action in my life and the lives of my family members. Parents can encourage their children for good or for evil. May I show them the course by word and example—that leads to the right choices.

NOURISH

"Yet he has not left himself without testimony:
He has shown kindness by giving you rain from
heaven and crops in their seasons; he provides you
with plenty of food and fills your hearts with joy."
ACTS 14:17 NIV

· · ·

Father, I looked out this morning to see a steady, soaking rain. I thought of my parched yard and how much the grass needed the precipitation. Within a few minutes, the blades of grass appeared green and glistened with life. Everything appears brighter and healthier after the rain.

Help me keep in mind, Lord, that it is my duty to nourish my children in all aspects of their lives. Lord, sometimes we become spiritually dry. Like a drought, the condition creeps in slowly over time. But Your Word refreshes our souls, strengthens us, and gives us spiritual growth.

Lord, help me constantly monitor the spiritual condition of my children and myself. Before our strength grows weak, please send heavenly water to refresh our souls and rejuvenate our worship. I pray that Your abundant blessings will continue to fall on my family and me.

GROWTH

Then he said to his disciples, "The harvest is plentiful,
but the laborers are few; therefore ask the Lord of the
harvest to send out laborers into his harvest."
MATTHEW 9:37–38 NRSV

■ ■ ■

Father, even from my limited gardening experience, I've seen that weeds grow without encouragement, but good crops require attention. Seeds must be planted in soil that has been prepared to receive them, the weeds must be eliminated, and the produce must be harvested at the right time.

Almighty Savior, I see that the same sequence is necessary to produce a harvest in the spiritual domain. Pull my sin out by the roots, and spiritually refresh me with the water of life.

Lord, as I embark upon the stage of my life as a father, I pray that I will be wise in ensuring that my children grow strong in Your love. Help me to be diligent in the work that brings my children to You. Lord, make me a faithful worker in Your harvest. May I have an urgency to gather them into Your kingdom before the season is past and Your crop is lost.

Vitamins

*My people are destroyed
for lack of knowledge.*
HOSEA 4:6 KJV

■ ■ ■

Heavenly Father, my doctor told me a dietary deficiency was causing a particular problem in my body. Despite healthy meals, some essential component was missing from my diet. The doctor recommended a minor change to what I ate, and the issue disappeared.

Father, if I search through Your Word and read only those passages that I find agreeable to my preconceived ideas of Your message, then I am missing some of the essential elements that I need for a strong relationship with You. I pray that I choose to become healthy by accepting all the spiritual vitamins that You have provided for me.

Lord, some diseases are not obvious to the eyes alone. As children grow to become young adults, they may have healthy bodies, but tragically, their lives are in turmoil because they have made wrong spiritual decisions. Please help me take care to nourish my children's lives with the full sustenance of the good news of Jesus.

OBEDIENCE

INDEPENDENCE

*"Then you will know the truth,
and the truth will set you free."*
JOHN 8:32 NIV

■ ■ ■

Heavenly Father, summer travel brochures always show a person on vacation strolling along a white sand beach, lying in a hammock, or watching a sunset. My vacations aren't as leisurely, and before they are over I look forward to returning to work. Independence Day is my favorite summer holiday because it has the good sense to last only one day—backyard barbecue, ball game, evening fireworks, and then it's over.

Thank You, Lord, for my personal independence day, the day You broke me away from sin so I could begin a personal, daily relationship with You.

Father, my children are always pushing for greater independence, and I do give them freedom that promotes growth. Because of the grounding that they have in faith, I am confident they are growing spiritually, too. May they see their growing independence as a reason to base more of their lives in obedience that brings them closer to You.

BOUNDARIES

Children, obey your parents in everything,
for this is your acceptable duty in the Lord. Fathers,
do not provoke your children, or they may lose heart.
COLOSSIANS 3:20–21 NRSV

■ ■ ■

Father, as I watch my young daughter coloring a picture, I see her tongue at the corner of her mouth and her face in deep concentration. She is determined not to go outside the lines. Finally, she manages to finish in triumph. I take it to hang in my office.

Lord, I am working to provide my daughter an environment that has reasonable boundaries and guidelines. If she works as hard staying within those boundaries as she does staying inside the lines of her coloring book, then she will be successful. But it took dozens of drawings before she succeeded at her coloring. I pray that I recognize her efforts to improve.

Father, I have not been able to control my life perfectly. Thank You for helping me get back within the boundaries You have set for me. May I be as patient with my children as You have been with me.

COMPLIANCE

But the steadfast love of the Lord is from everlasting to everlasting on those who fear him, and his righteousness to children's children, to those who keep his covenant and remember to do his commandments.
PSALM 103:17–18 NRSV

■ ■ ■

Father, when it is time for my children to leave a playground, I give the final call and start for the car. They come, but at a snail's pace. They drag their feet and divert from one piece of playground equipment along their path to the next. They pretend they are obeying my call, but their actions show otherwise. I explain to them that delay or an excessively slow response is not obedience.

Lord, how many times have You seen my obedience in this way? I say I will do something, but I find ways to put it off or accomplish it a piece at a time without giving it my earnest effort.

Father, children who do not listen to their parents often end up in difficult circumstances. Yet I sometimes find myself being as deaf to Your commands as my children are to mine. Please forgive my slow response and childish attempts to avoid the work You have given me.

Enthusiasm

For by thee I have run through a troop:
by my God have I leaped over a wall.
2 Samuel 22:30 KJV

■ ■ ■

Father, I wish to develop a trusting acceptance of Your
will. Grant me the willingness to accept Your plans for me
with obedient enthusiasm.

Lord, I recognize the need for a strong faith, but may
I never try to impose my human will on Your sovereign
power. Sometimes I come before You in prayer with an
agenda of things that I think needs done. I look at the list
and toss it aside. What do I know about Your intention for
my life? It is not my demands that need addressed but
Your will. Grant me the willingness to trust and accept
Your purpose.

Father, You still have faith in me after all the times
that I have failed to show a strong faith in You. I pray that
I continue to grow in faith and to shape my life according
to Your will. May my family see not only that I do have
faith but also that I shape my life by it.

PATIENCE

LEARNING

The seed is the word of God. But that on the good ground are they, which in an honest and good heart, having heard the word, keep it, and bring forth fruit with patience.
LUKE 8:11, 15 KJV

■ ■ ■

Father, my son was supposed to wait for the carpool to hockey practice, but when they called to say they would be late, he decided to ride his bike. He carried his hockey stick across the handlebars. He took a tumble when the stick caught on a sign. Later, I asked what had caused the accident. He thought for a moment and gave the correct answer—impatience.

Lord, like my son, I often lack patience. I can usually trace lost opportunities and troubles to being impatient. Often, the object that gains my attention and to which I run is not important enough to justify the effort.

Father, help me reschedule my life so I can let go of the lesser things. May I seize the important values that should rule my life. I am thankful that You see my impatient mistakes—and help me out of them. You help me grow into a stronger, more patient person.

SPECIAL

*Finally, brothers and sisters, whatever is true, whatever
is noble, whatever is right, whatever is pure, whatever
is lovely, whatever is admirable—if anything is excellent
or praiseworthy—think about such things.*
PHILIPPIANS 4:8 NIV

■ ■ ■

Father, I took my family on a glass-bottom boat tour of
coral reefs. The tour guide told us that it took many years
for tiny organisms to develop the colorful coral reefs that
we could view through the underwater windows.

Lord, thank You for Your creation. Some things I can
readily see, but others are hidden from ordinary vision.
As I look at other people, direct me to realize that I cannot
always see the work You are doing in their lives. Give me
patience to look for the things that are good in others.

Father, I know that Your creative power is still shap-
ing individuals to become more like You. Like the coral
reef that is difficult to see under the ocean's surface,
desirable qualities are sometimes difficult to see in others. Take away from me any judgmental spirit. Adjust my
thoughts and the thoughts of my children to think on the
worth You have placed on each individual person.

WILLPOWER

For bodily exercise profiteth little: but godliness
is profitable unto all things, having promise of the
life that now is, and of that which is to come.
1 TIMOTHY 4:8 KJV

■ ■ ■

Father, along with getting older has come an expanding waistline. Controlling my weight is a constant challenge. I exercise regularly and am selective of the foods I eat, but maintaining a healthy weight is still a problem. The Bible reassures us that You are not as concerned with our outward appearance as You are with the condition of our hearts.

Lord, help me to direct my children to feast on the spiritual food of Your Word. Give them the willpower to overcome evil and temptations that would weaken their witness for You. As my children grow into adulthood, develop in them the characteristics that will make them beautiful for You.

Father, help me pursue these worthy goals knowing that I do not achieve them by brief effort but by lifelong commitment to a righteous course of action. Lord, my prayer is that daily You will transform me to live a life that will bring honor to You.

Sacrifice

*For our light affliction, which is but for
a moment, worketh for us a far more
exceeding and eternal weight of glory.*
2 Corinthians 4:17 kjv

■ ■ ■

Father, I must visit the dentist far more often now because I avoided dental care in my early years. When I was younger, I put off as long as possible what I hoped I could get out of doing altogether. But a few minutes of discomfort in the dentist's chair back then would have guarded against hours of toothache today. I chose to avoid the dentist, and now I pay the price.

Lord, I am thankful that this distressing pattern has not developed in my children. Whether it's from my negative example or better character traits acquired from their mother, my children appear to be following a better way.

Lord, help me exercise good judgment to accept the sacrifice that it takes to be a true Christian. I know that my efforts are minor compared to the rewards that await me in the future life.

PRAYER

CONTROLLED

*"Then you will call on me and come and pray to me,
and I will listen to you. You will seek me and find
me when you seek me with all your heart."*
JEREMIAH 29:12–13 NIV

■ ■ ■

Father, I have a friend, an airplane pilot, who has an instrument flight rating. When dark clouds surround him, when all visual contact with the ground is lost, he continues on by relying on the airplane's instruments and the directions given by air traffic controllers. He has been trained not merely to read the instruments but to trust them even when he becomes disoriented.

Lord, sometimes the troubles of this world surround me. I become spiritually disoriented. To avoid disaster, I must direct my course by talking to You in prayer and accepting Your Word as the guide to get me through the dark times.

Father, my children have come to me tilted from their equilibrium by the conflicting messages of the world. Direct me in how to point them to You as the Master of their lives. They will stay on course only by putting themselves under the control of Your higher authority.

Authentic

*I do not cease to give thanks for you as I remember
you in my prayers. I pray that the God of our Lord
Jesus Christ, the Father of glory, may give you a spirit
of wisdom and revelation as you come to know him.*
Ephesians 1:16–17 NRSV

. . .

Father, I face many challenges in my Christian walk.
These challenges can be overcome with prayers that spe-
cifically address what is troubling me. Often, my prayers
fail because I sink into a rote pattern. I am merely mouth-
ing words but do not take up the authentic issues at the
core of my concern. I do not address what is, or should be,
on my heart.

Lord, when I read Your Word, I find prayers by the
heroes of faith—Moses, Joshua, David, Peter, Paul, and
many others. They prayed for wisdom, confidence, guidance, boldness, restoration, healing, and safekeeping.
They prayed during a time of crisis, and their prayers
went to the heart of the matter.

Father, I seek Your blessings in the practical, day-
to-day issues of my life—my joys, fears, and aspirations.
I pray that I will study Your Word so that it serves as a
launching point into a deeper, more forceful prayer time.

HEAVEN'S GATE

*Keep yourselves in the love of God, looking for the
mercy of our Lord Jesus Christ unto eternal life.*
JUDE 21 KJV

■ ■ ■

Father, after I became an adult, my father influenced me
more than any other person in my life. As his life drew to
a close, we knew that he would soon leave this world for a
better one. I remember an airplane flight that mirrored my
feelings. As the airplane descended into clouds for land-
ing, the ride became bumpy. The plane shook as the lash-
ing rain buffeted it. But after we dipped below the clouds
and touched down, the setting sun illuminated everything
with a warm glow. At the gate, my family welcomed me
home.

Lord, like the airplane flight, a few bumps have reminded me of how blessed the rest of my life has been.
When I arrive at my final destination, I will be illuminated
by Your light. Those who have gone before me, including
my mother and father, will be there welcoming me home.
Lord, help me prepare for living at home forever with You.

BLESSINGS

"Stand up and praise the LORD your God, who is from everlasting to everlasting." "Blessed be your glorious name, and may it be exalted above all blessing and praise."
NEHEMIAH 9:5 NIV

...

Father, I come to spend some time with You in conversation. Today, I wish to express my thanks for all You have done for me. You have provided me with a loving family, and we have enjoyed Your protection and blessings.

Lord, I know that all good things come from You. Sometimes I think only of the things I have as indications of blessings. I am guilty of looking with the green eyes of envy at others who appear to have received richer portions. But often when their situation is fully revealed, I have no desire to trade any part of my life with them. Open my eyes to see that the things I do not have would be detrimental to my relationship with You.

Father, I pray that I can always express my love for You and my thankfulness for Your blessings in my life.

PROTECTION

SAFETY

*"Because the poor are plundered and the needy groan,
I will now arise," says the LORD. "I will protect them
from those who malign them." And the words of the
LORD are flawless, like silver purified in a crucible,
like gold refined seven times. You, LORD, will keep the
needy safe and will protect us forever from the wicked.*
PSALM 12:5–7 NIV

■ ■ ■

Lord, raising a family is a daunting task. Just as I learn
what is required for children at a certain age, they grow
older, and an entirely different set of skills is needed. But
in all stages of their lives, I must offer my children patience, understanding, wisdom, and protection. Equip me
in abundance with the characteristics I need to provide for
them and keep them safe. I ask for Your constant help and
boundless compassion.

Father, I see my role as a shepherd. Not only must I
lead my family in the right direction, I must also protect
them from the evil that will attempt to snatch them away.
I want my children to have a loving home that is a place of
safety where they are always welcome.

GUARDIAN

Behold, the angel of the Lord appeareth to Joseph in a
dream, saying, Arise, and take the young child and his
mother, and flee into Egypt, and be thou there until I bring
thee word: for Herod will seek the young child to destroy
him. When he arose, he took the young child and his
mother by night, and departed into Egypt.
MATTHEW 2:13–14 KJV

...

Father, I know of children who have been placed in the
care of a guardian. I admire men who can step in and
take over the duties of a father to children who do not
biologically belong to them. In many cases, the father
has missed the formative years in which the child is most
easily molded. An adopted or foster child has added emotional baggage because of frequent moves and unstable
situations. Acting as an adoptive or foster father is an
enormous task!

Lord, I think of Joseph, who took on the role of being
the father of Jesus. Because of the threats to the newborn
baby, Joseph willingly uprooted his family and escaped to
a distant country.

Father, I pray that I am willing to make the sacrifices
to ensure that my family is protected from the evil in this
world.

EXAGGERATION

I have seen all the works that are done under the sun;
and, behold, all is vanity and vexation of spirit.
ECCLESIASTES 1:14 KJV

■ ■ ■

Father, each day I am bombarded with advertisements. I am assured that the merchandise is on the leading edge. I suddenly discover a product is essential although I have been getting along without it all of my life. I disparage as outdated my perfectly serviceable possessions.

Lord, advertisements target each one of my family members regardless of our ages. I am concerned that my younger children may believe that eating a certain cereal will give them amazing physical powers. I cringe as glamorous fashion models assure my older daughter that a certain shampoo will change her life. Help me protect them from these exaggerated claims.

Heavenly Father, I pray that my family and I will not allow advertisements to encourage our tendency to be discontent. Help us dismiss sales pitches that appeal to desire and pride. Keep us away from the idea that we can improve our future with things rather than living right for You.

VALUES

■ ■ ■

Lord, every day my eyes and ears are beset with those who
want to bend my will to their purposes. Testimonies from
famous personalities, glittering television advertisements,
and half-truths of insincere politicians are all trying to
muddle my reasoning so I cannot distinguish between truth
and lies. They want us to listen and not ask questions. I try
to protect my children from the glitzy advertising and forceful efforts that assail their eyes and ears.

I am well aware that many advertisers attack a person's basic convictions with persuasive arguments in
order to substitute alternate beliefs. My children come
under the influence of those who attempt to program their
minds. Father, help me use the abilities You have given
me to carefully evaluate the claims made by those who
are trying to influence me. Help me teach my children to
use all the abilities You have given them to separate the
false from the true.

♥

GIVING

The plans of the diligent lead to profit
as surely as haste leads to poverty.
PROVERBS 21:5 NIV

■ ■ ■

Father, with the start of each new school year, I can look forward to my school-age children being involved in a variety of fund-raising projects. They range from offering to do yard work, to the walks for this or that cause, to the selling of nutrition-questionable boxes of candy.

Lord, it seems every cause has a compelling reason why I should support the effort. I find it difficult to separate the vital few from the trivial many. I cannot learn enough about every group's programs to fully support what they are doing. Give me the wisdom to direct my support to those who are carrying out Your will. I pray I will always be willing to make sacrifices, but keep me from being a wasteful giver.

Heavenly Father, You have abundantly blessed me. Guide me to practical ways that I can be a benefit to those who are doing Your will.

WEALTH

Let your conversation be without covetousness;
and be content with such things as ye have: for he
hath said, I will never leave thee, nor forsake thee.
HEBREWS 13:5 KJV

· · ·

Dear Lord, You know I worry about money. Not because I am afraid I will not have enough, but because of my concern for those who depend upon me. I feel a strong obligation to provide for my family.

Father, help me understand the joy of honest effort and the emptiness of gain by dishonest means. Remind me that piling up wealth for wealth alone casts a gloomy shadow over a person's life. May I realize that what I do have far exceeds what I do not have. I pray for abundance of the heart and not of possession.

Lord, prevent me from using my role as a provider to rationalize an excessive devotion to making money. I pray that I will never measure success by material wealth or possessions or think of money as a symbol of my virility. Thank You for assuring me that You will fulfill the needs of my family.

Just in Time

Now he who supplies seed to the sower and bread for food will
also supply and increase your store of seed and will enlarge
the harvest of your righteousness. You will be enriched in
every way so that you can be generous on every occasion,
and through us your generosity will result in thanksgiving to God.
2 Corinthians 9:10–11 niv

. . .

Father, at one time, I worked for a company that had a
"just in time" inventory system. Computers tracked sales
and ordered additional stock at the right moment to re-
plenish what was needed.

Lord, I know that You are far more dependable than
any system devised by humankind. But You know that
I struggle to avoid needless worry, especially when it
comes to events affecting my family.

All of my past experience shows me that You always
grant what I need when I need it. The supply is always
there at the right moment. Remind me to put aside my
needless worry and instead concentrate on living with the
confidence that You will provide.

LIVING WATER

"Let anyone who is thirsty come to me and drink.
Whoever believes in me, as Scripture has said,
rivers of living water will flow from within them."
JOHN 7:37–38 NIV

■ ■ ■

Father, while traveling in desert country, I was surprised to come across a group of people going scuba diving. One of the small communities had grown up around a huge natural spring. The spring's source offered a place to make deep dives in the middle of a dry climate. The constant flow of water turned nearby fields green. The spring gave life to the desert and drew travelers to it.

Lord, in the Bible, Jesus describes Himself as "living water." I trust that my family and I will always gather around the source of eternal life to refresh our spirits. You are the One who brings life to the branches.

Father, the hardest of soil can be made fertile, and the driest of grass can be made green when water is available. Help me be a refreshing example of Your living water to others.

RESPECT

*Moreover, we had human parents to discipline us,
and we respected them. Should we not be even more
willing to be subject to the Father of spirits and live?*
HEBREWS 12:9 NRSV

■ ■ ■

Lord, although I do not often acknowledge it, I realize that
the respect of my family is important to me. I see other
men who are devastated when they lose the respect of
someone they cherish. I have heard that for some fathers,
being respected by their families is more important than
being loved. "Not me, Lord," I say. But I know I can be
shattered by a word rashly spoken, especially by my wife,
or by my children when I sense that they view some aspect
of my personality in less than flattering terms.

Father, I know that it is impossible to please everyone. But I do wish to be highly regarded by my family and
by those whose opinions are important to me. I pray that
I inspire respect by serving and by making sacrifices. Remove from me the concern that my sense of purpose depends on how others view me. Replace it with my concern
with how You regard me.

LEADERSHIP

At Caesarea there was a man named Cornelius,
a centurion in what was known as the Italian Regiment.
He and all his family were devout and God-fearing; he gave
generously to those in need and prayed to God regularly.
ACTS 10:1–2 NIV

■■■

Lord, sometimes I look around and see all kinds of sin in this world. I let my guard down, and I am tempted to say or do something I know is wrong. In a moment like that, I remember the account of Noah. He refused to compromise his righteous walk with You, Lord.

In the Bible, I read how the righteousness of a father influenced those around him. Cornelius, the centurion, and his entire family are described as "devout." As a father, I want to lead my whole family to You and keep them in fellowship with You.

Dear God, help me to find favor in the eyes of those around me and especially in Your eyes by maintaining Christian traits. The most important concern in my life is that my family and I will please You.

INTEGRITY

*He kneeled upon his knees three times a day, and prayed,
and gave thanks before his God, as he did aforetime.*
DANIEL 6:10 KJV

■ ■ ■

Lord, I want to live an upright life no matter how difficult
the circumstances. I look to Daniel as an example of one
who was not afraid to do what was right, even though he
faced death in a den of lions. You gave him protection
and blessed his integrity.

Heavenly Father, I want to be like Daniel, who held
fast to his faith despite great demands to do otherwise.
His story strengthens me, and I pray that it will also
strengthen my children as they mature and go out into the
world. When they face tough times, I pray they will continue to put their trust in You.

O Lord, in reading about Daniel, I see how he devoted
himself to prayer and thanksgiving. Give me a strong faith
to share with my family. You are more powerful than any
enemies of my soul, and You have every situation of my
life under control.

WONDER

O LORD, how manifold are thy works! in wisdom hast
thou made them all: the earth is full of thy riches.
PSALM 104:24 KJV

■ ■ ■

Lord, Your creation provokes a sense of wonder in me.
From the rocky shores with crashing surf to a humid rain-
forest with water dripping from the trees, the range of
Your creation is beyond comprehension. I feel the same
wonder when I read from Your Word. It contains wonderful poetry and soul-stirring songs. I read in it exciting
stories of the heroes of faith. I marvel at miraculous events
that are beyond human comprehension. Each day of reading the Bible is a new adventure and a wonderful journey.
Holy scripture is a light that guides me to righteousness.

Lord, I pray that I can instill in my children a sense
of wonder in Your creation and Your Word. I pray that for
them and for me, Your Word will always be fresh and will
illuminate our lives. I pray that we will read Your Word,
contemplate Your message, and keep it in our minds
throughout each day.

ROLE MODEL

PERFECTION

*Do not conform to the pattern of this world,
but be transformed by the renewing of your mind.
Then you will be able to test and approve what
God's will is—his good, pleasing and perfect will.*
ROMANS 12:2 NIV

■ ■ ■

Father, through You, I know the qualities a good father should possess. I am thankful that I have You as a model of what I should be. Qualities like kindness, selflessness, reassurance, and attentiveness are just a few. But I know that children do not always experience the love and care that You intend for us as fathers to provide.

Lord, to have the authority to direct my household in the ways of righteousness and truth, my family must recognize me as being an example of one who does Your will. Only by my study of the Bible, frequent conversation with You, and thankfulness for Your blessings will they have confidence that I know what I am doing.

Father, guide me as I faithfully train my children. I desire to show them a consistent pattern of what it means to be a loving father. Because I cannot measure up to perfection, I pray that they will look beyond me to You.

Hero

For this slight momentary affliction is preparing us for an eternal weight of glory beyond all measure, because we look not at what can be seen but at what cannot be seen; for what can be seen is temporary, but what cannot be seen is eternal.
2 Corinthians 4:17–18 NRSV

■ ■ ■

Father, while working out at the gym, I've seen people wearing shirts with a professional athlete's name and jersey number. The writing shows whom they admire.

Lord, I am not an athlete, so others are unlikely to wear a shirt with my name on it. But I simply desire that the characteristics my family and others see in me will be those of a faithful Christian. Help me express to my children that earthly fame is temporary, but Christian principals are eternal.

Father, help my children become aware that the outward persona of a person may conceal a character that is not worthy of admiration. I pray that they will never become so enamored with a public figure that they are shattered when their hero is revealed to have failed. Instead, I pray that they emulate the One who never fails and acknowledge You above all others.

INFLUENCE

Hold to the standard of sound teaching that you
have heard from me, in the faith and love that are
in Christ Jesus. Guard the good treasure entrusted
to you, with the help of the Holy Spirit living in us.
2 TIMOTHY 1:13–14 NRSV

■ ■ ■

Father, when in a boat, I am surprised at the strength of the waves generated by other boats. A vessel may be well away from me and pass at slow speed. The boat seems to produce a gentle swell on the water, but the waves strike my boat with a solid slapping sound that reveals their full power. The waves can continue to rock my boat long after the vessel that caused them has passed.

Lord, I understand that the way I conduct my life can also have a far-reaching influence. Consequences may only become apparent long after my efforts have ended.

Father, I pray that others feel my influence and that it is a positive one. Lord, help me communicate Your love to my children by my relationship with You and by my compassion for others. Guide me in the way of righteousness.

WALK WITH GOD

Noah was a righteous man, blameless among
the people of his time, and he walked faithfully with God.
GENESIS 6:9 NIV

■ ■ ■

Lord, I am largely defined by those whom I choose as heroes and models for my life. Others interpret my character by the characters of those with whom I walk. I want to be like the heroes of old, those men of renown in the Bible, who were described as having "walked with God."

Dear Father, give me the determination to walk at Your side. I seek an honorable walk that shows Your power and character. I know that I am not walking alone; You are with me. I have the victory over impossible circumstances because I have placed myself in Your footsteps.

Father, I pray, too, that my children recognize that their choices of friends will profoundly affect their lives. Help me provide them the opportunity to develop friendships with those who share the vision to be effective Christians.

TEACHING

SPIRITUAL EDUCATION

You therefore, beloved, since you are forewarned, beware that you are not carried away with the error of the lawless and lose your own stability. But grow in the grace and knowledge of our Lord and Savior Jesus Christ. To him be the glory both now and to the day of eternity. Amen.

2 PETER 3:17–18 NRSV

. . .

Father, I am struck by the fact that despite the wealth of a great nation, citizens with an inferior education may live as if they were in an underdeveloped country. Often, I fail to understand that this principle applies to my spiritual life, as well.

Lord, my family and I are blessed with so many ways to delve deeply into Your Word. The Bible is available in both paper and electronic form. Bible dictionaries and other aids for studying scripture abound in many editions. Dedicated teachers conduct Bible studies tailored for every age group and level of expertise. I pray, dear Father, that we will take advantage of these opportunities to have a world-class spiritual education so that we eliminate the poverty of spiritual ignorance.

Heavenly Father, open my eyes to opportunities to have family devotions. I resolve to read the Bible, pray, and have a short devotion together sometime each day.

DIRECTIONS

All scripture is inspired by God and is useful for teaching,
for reproof, for correction, and for training in
righteousness, so that everyone who belongs to God
may be proficient, equipped for every good work.
2 TIMOTHY 3:16–17 NRSV

■ ■ ■

Father, I spent the morning trying to put together the barbecue grill, which was labeled, "Some assembly required." If I had read the directions to begin with, it would have been simpler—maybe. Even when I did bring myself to read the directions, I couldn't figure out what was required of me.

Lord, sometimes I try to put my life together without reading Your directions. Thank You for providing a clear set of directions for life. Thankfully, I can read Your Word and understand the principles that make me—Your creation—function correctly.

Father, I want my children to also understand the benefits of having daily guidance from Your Word. A well-read Bible in my hands is a powerful example to my children of its importance. Build our faith that You have the answers when we face life's questions. Please guide us to Your Word before we become confused by the world's ineffective counsel.

MENTOR

■ ■ ■

Father, I occasionally take on the role of a teacher, although I often feel inadequate for the task. My goal is to be a mentor, guide, and advisor. May I grow in knowledge, wisdom, character, and confidence so I can help those whom I teach to choose the proper path.

Lord, as a father, I want to encourage my children to study for careers that match their abilities. I also desire for them to decide to serve You in every aspect of their lives. Give me the talent to instill in them the realization that worship of You is a daily activity that includes all aspects of their lives, including their jobs.

Heavenly Teacher, provide me with the ability to instill in my children a love for learning more about You, reading the Bible, talking to You in prayer, and living a life in keeping with Your Word. May I have an influence that will last a lifetime.

EXAMPLE

For I have given you an example,
that ye should do as I have done to you.
JOHN 13:15 KJV

■ ■ ■

"Model the ideal behavior," a supervisor told me when I was taking a class to train others. "Show examples of the skill you want to transfer to the other employees, and give them guided practice." I found that neither textbook nor lecture taught as well as a real-life demonstration.

Heavenly Father, I appreciate reading about the life of Your Son and seeing how He taught the world about Your love through His examples and teaching. He portrayed compassion by healing the sick and feeding the multitudes. He expressed the depth of Your forgiveness by giving His life for my sins.

Lord, now it is time for me to model the right behavior for my family. I cannot delegate to others the lifesaving spiritual examples my children need. I need to communicate Your teachings by a wholesome life and genuine love for You. May they see my joy in serving You so that they, too, are drawn to You.

TRUST

OPEN MIND

Train up a child in the way he should go:
and when he is old, he will not depart from it.
PROVERBS 22:6 KJV

■ ■ ■

Father, my young son is at a wonderful age. Each morning I think about some new skill that I saw him display the previous day. Each night I delight in watching him throw himself into learning a new task. From climbing onto a chair, walking down stairs, tossing a ball, or stacking blocks, he attacks it with enthusiasm. I am both astonished and pleased at how fast the little one is developing.

Lord, I've seen birds in a nest open their mouths, ready to take whatever their parents deliver for them to eat. They fully trust their parents and never think that it might do them harm.

Father, it is a tremendous responsibility You have given me to raise my children. May I always be aware that their minds are as quick to absorb new information as their bodies are to learn new skills. Guide me as I put into their hearts the unwavering conviction that they can always trust You.

FEARLESS

*But now, this is what the L*ORD *says—he who created you,*
Jacob, he who formed you, Israel: "Do not fear, for I have
redeemed you; I have summoned you by name; you are mine."
ISAIAH 43:1 NIV

■ ■ ■

Father, when I prayed for You to quell the doubts and fears that troubled my mind, You helped me to overcome those events that were in my power to change. You gave me the emotional soundness to bear those trials that remained. I see now that You put them there so that by enduring them I would gain character and confidence.

Lord, You have given me experiences that improved my abilities as a father. If I will be guided by You, ask for advice from Christians who embrace Your wisdom, and pray to implement what I have learned, then I will be able to be a father that my children can trust.

Heavenly Father, help me recognize the distress of others when they are in the valley. Let me support them through their dark days. Give me the wisdom to be an encouragement to them. May I learn to put my trust in You and succeed in sharing that trust with others.

PROTECTION

He is like a man which built an house, and digged deep,
and laid the foundation on a rock: and when the flood arose,
the stream beat vehemently upon that house, and could
not shake it: for it was founded upon a rock.
LUKE 6:48 KJV

■ ■ ■

Dear Lord, as a young child, my walk home from a friend's house took me through a small patch of woods. This particular grove always appeared exceptionally dark. The moist earth around the roots carried an unpleasant dank smell. I would pull my coat around me and hurry through while I tried to act more brave than I actually felt.

Father, as my children grow older, the time comes for them to take small steps of their own into the world. Dangers, especially spiritual ones, are all around us. Please protect them in their journeys. I pray they put on Your robe of righteousness so Satan cannot harm them.

Jesus, I'm traveling through a realm where You have given Satan access. Although this world is not my final destination, I must pass through it while on my way home. I pray for You to cover me and surround me with Your atoning blood.

DANGEROUSLY DEAD

Trust ye in the LORD for ever: for in the
LORD JEHOVAH is everlasting strength.
ISAIAH 26:4 KJV

■ ■ ■

Father, the great oak tree had become dangerously dead, but no one could tell. The death was in the heartwood, working from the inside out. When the storm came, the trunk snapped, fell, and crushed smaller trees nearby.

Lord, sometimes I have become captivated by people whom I considered towering Christians. But I could not see their hearts, and occasionally their lives collapsed because they had become but a shell of Christianity. When they fell, I became disillusioned. I pray that my trust will always be upon You as my ultimate, unfailing leader.

Father, I pray that my children understand that the only true role model for them is Jesus. It is easy for them to look up to adults who later prove to be less than worthy of their admiration. Guide me to help them understand that You are the only One who will never fail them.

VICTORY

CORNERSTONE

"See, I am laying in Zion a stone,
a cornerstone chosen and precious;
and whoever believes in him will not be put to shame."
1 PETER 2:6 NRSV

∎ ∎ ∎

Heavenly Father, yesterday I helped as my little girl put together a puzzle. At first, the pieces were all mixed together without a pattern. It was confusing to her, and she didn't know where to start. I showed her one of the corner pieces. After she had that piece in place, one by one she succeeded in fitting the others together.

Lord, before I gave my heart to You and sought Your will, my life was a confusing collection of parts. But as I developed a personal relationship with You, a clearer image formed of what You have in store for me. I saw that putting my life back together became easier once I chose You as my starting point.

Although my daughter's future is not yet fully revealed, I pray that she will gladly put the disarrayed components of her life in Your hands to complete the picture.

Roots

. . .

Father, weeds in my yard resisted my efforts to eradicate them. Cutting them down at grass-top level did not destroy them. They merely grew back. Stronger methods were needed, such as digging the roots out by hand.

Lord, sometimes I have problems in my life that I treat too lightly. I mask the symptoms at the surface level without looking for the cause that goes deeper. The problems reappear because I have not attacked the root of them. Help me find lasting answers to those things that should not be in my life.

Father, let me recognize in myself and in my children those habits that allow sin to take root. Rescue us and help us weed out by the roots rebellion, apathy, resentment, and destructive tendencies. Help us be effective in replacing them with love, joy, peace, patience, and all the fruit of the Holy Spirit.

PREVAIL

For the love of God is this, that we obey his commandments.
And his commandments are not burdensome, for whatever
is born of God conquers the world. And this is the victory
that conquers the world, our faith.

1 JOHN 5:3–4 NRSV

■ ■ ■

Father, I often take too long to weigh the pros and cons of a situation. Help me quickly recognize and eliminate those choices that are outside the Christian realm. I want to overcome the evil in my life.

I can only be defeated because I am inconsistent in my dedication to You. I hesitate when I should press the attack. Give me the determination to serve only You and the faith to stand firmly on the side of righteousness.

Lord, through my lack of perseverance, my children can become the innocent victims of heartless evil. Protect them when my protection grows weak.

Father, I want to master the adversary and bring my evil desires into submission. Give me the strength to prevail whether it is a swift victory or a prolonged battle. May I never view success as the end of the struggle, but instead remain vigilant to the ongoing efforts of Satan to thwart Your plan for my life.

SERVICE

I can do all things through
Christ which strengtheneth me.
PHILIPPIANS 4:13 KJV

■ ■ ■

Father, I go out each day as a soldier for You. If I am rewarded with victory after victory, may I examine my goals in case I am aiming too low. Teach me to see clearly the battles You want me to fight. Give me the ability to think the impossible, and fill me with the aggressive faith to make it happen.

Lord, may I never use my understanding of Your commands to launch a personal attack on individuals. I want to firmly stand for what is right and do so in such a way that Your love dominates the situation. Help me instill in my children the understanding that we must follow Your will despite what others might be doing.

Father, battles are long and victories are short. I would rather enjoy victories than failure, but I would rather suffer a lost battle than stand on the sidelines doing nothing. Almighty God, I surrender myself to Your service.

RESIST

Submit yourselves therefore to God.
Resist the devil, and he will flee from you.
JAMES 4:7 KJV

■ ■ ■

Lord, my visits to the zoo with my children always include a tour through the reptile house. The boa constrictor is big and strong. The poisonous rattlesnake imparts fear by the warning rattle of its tail. At first, the snakes repelled my children, but as their fear diminished, they became fascinated by them. They put their faces close to the glass to see every detail.

Father, a walk by the snakes reminds me of the analogy of Satan to a serpent. I explain to my children that unlike reptiles that avoid humans and strike only because they feel danger is near, Satan hunts victims to attack. I reminded them that sin could also lure them closer. At first sin repels them, but should they grow accustomed to it, they could be easily enticed to participate in it.

Protective Lord, thank You for the promise that we can have victory over Satan by resisting him through Your name.

ROAD MAP

"I will lead the blind by ways they have not known, along unfamiliar paths I will guide them; I will turn the darkness into light before them and make the rough places smooth. These are the things I will do; I will not forsake them."
ISAIAH 42:16 NIV

■ ■ ■

Lord, I plan a driving trip in exhaustive detail, highlighting the best route on the map, pinning down stopovers, and identifying points of interest. All of this requires a great deal of study that begins weeks before the departure date. Shortly before we leave, I check the car's oil and other fluids and the air pressure in the tires. After we pack and are ready to go, I make sure the baby is in his car seat and everyone is securely buckled. I do not want anything to go wrong.

Father, I pray that I take even more care in planning my heavenly trip. I don't know how much time I have to prepare for it, but while there is still time, I will talk to You in prayer, study the Bible to learn Your will, and work to be a faithful servant. I pray that my concern to secure my children's physical safety is only exceeded by my efforts for their spiritual well-being.

PLEASING PATTERNS

Whatever you have learned or received or heard
from me, or seen in me—put it into practice.
And the God of peace will be with you.
PHILIPPIANS 4:9 NIV

■ ■ ■

Father, frequent repetition causes me to acquire a behavior that becomes an unconscious habit. When I fall into a habit and allow my conscious mind to give up its responsibilities, I glide through the activity without really thinking.

Lord, it seems the habits that I pick up most readily are the bad ones. In Your Word, I read to guard against bad habits such as failing to meet with other Christians and being idle. I mistrust a habit because it is an action without thinking. So I pray that I am always mindful of what I am doing. Only then can I assess whether I am following Your will and making the right choices. I want to develop acceptable practices and help my children do the same.

Help me, Father, exchange these old eyes for new ones. Let me look at my life and recognize unconscious habits, especially the bad ones. Help me change them into a conscious pattern pleasing to You.

COBWEBS

He lies in wait near the villages; from ambush he murders
the innocent, His eyes watch in secret for his victims.
PSALM 10:8 NIV

■ ■ ■

Heavenly Father, spiders spin webs to snare wandering insects. They are found in most locations worldwide. I have seen spider webs in obscure places, and I wonder why an insect would ever be trapped. But the spider knows how to capture unsuspecting victims.

Father, I know that Satan, too, catches valuable souls in a web of sin. Often the temptation is placed in an unsuspecting location. Like spiders, he spins his web of deceit worldwide. His influence can be found in all places.

Lord, guard my mind, body, and spirit from Satan's lures. Deliver me from the temptation to violate Your laws. Only with Your help can I maintain a holy lifestyle and avoid becoming a victim seized by deception. My children are appealing targets for the forces of destruction. Protect them against the lure of Satan that would wrap them in the sticky web of sin.

LIFETIME LOVE

Each of you, however, should love his wife as himself,
and a wife should respect her husband.
EPHESIANS 5:33 NRSV

■ ■ ■

Lord, I've heard that a husband prays for You to keep his wife the sweet person he married, and a wife prays for You to change her husband into the man she wants him to be. Instead, I will pray that You make us what You want us to be.

Father, I ask You to strengthen my wife in the many tasks that are part of being a mother to our children. I pray that we work together to make the right decisions in raising them. Looking ahead, may we always keep in mind that after they have left home, our love for one another will not have diminished but instead will have grown richer from the experience.

I am thankful, Lord, that I married the woman I loved, and today I can say I love the woman I married. I pray that I will respect her as a faithful partner, and we will walk side by side in the path You direct.

Captivated

*May your fountain be blessed, and may you rejoice in the wife
of your youth. A loving doe, a graceful deer—may her breasts
satisfy you always, may you ever be intoxicated with her love.*
PROVERBS 5:18–19 NIV

* * *

Father, thank You for revealing the loveliness of my wife
to me. I can see You in her actions. At the end of a trying day, she still shows sweet patience with our children.
She consoles an upset child as if his ache were all that
mattered. She makes pain go away merely by her sooth-
ing kiss. She does the same for me. She sees bravery,
strength, and ability when I see none of those heroic qualities. She is the most beautiful person in my life.

Lord, for some people, love is a thunderstorm—
intense but of short duration. Encourage our enthusiasm
for one another so that it endures. I pray that our love is
everlasting, earnest, and selfless.

Father, I want to care for my wife, embrace her, and
cherish her. May I continue to develop a oneness with her
that I share with no other person. I pray that we create a
future where we act in agreement with our shared hopes
and dreams.

BOND

■ ■ ■

Father, I pray that my wife and I will show one another the love You have shown to us. May we be bound together in affection—two minds with but a single mission. When we work together toward spiritual goals, we feel our love for one another and for You stronger than on any other occasion. May we complement and complete one another so our separate, personal goals combine to become a single effort to serve You.

Lord, our victories have not all been won, but together we press ahead. We have so much in common—a common love for You and for our children and a determination to live lives worthy of one another's respect.

Father, I am confident that my wife and I are dedicated to bringing our lives into alignment with Your will. May we speak often with You, study Your Word, live in Your assurance, and pursue Your righteousness.

HARMONY

May the God of steadfastness and encouragement
grant you to live in harmony with one another, in accordance
with Christ Jesus, so that together you may with one voice
glorify the God and Father of our Lord Jesus Christ.
ROMANS 15:5–6 NRSV

■ ■ ■

Father, I want for my wife and me to live in the union of Your love. Help us develop the trust to share with one another all of our fears, hopes, and dreams. May we always rejoice in one another's victories and mitigate one another's failures. Guide us to work together to overcome problems that our marriage may encounter.

Lord, my wife is a delight to me. When I experience sorrow, she shares the sadness but draws me out to joy. When I am dejected, she makes me cheerful. She fills my heart with optimism.

Father, grant me the sensitivity to recognize when discord and distance begin to separate us. I pray that I'll never let a moment of reckless folly drive a wedge of sin between us. I put myself under Your control and sacrifice my personal motives to bring harmony to my marriage.